The Disciple Investing Apostle

Changed Lives Changing Lives
SERIES PREFACE

The "Changed Lives Changing Lives" series contains three books that cover the ministry of Christian "disciple investing." As a series, the books address the following aspects of pouring into followers and disciples of Jesus: methodology (*The "Disciple Investing" Life*), philosophy (*Christ Changing Lives*) and relational modeling (*The "Disciple Investing" Apostle*). Whether you are a novice in ministering to others, a seasoned veteran in Christian education, or looking for some inspiration to gain motivation for sharing your life on behalf of others, the "Changed Lives Changing Lives" series is here to help. The author's hope is that the reader will benefit from each book in the series, and that the kingdom of Christ will benefit from the fruit of the changed lives of impacted "disciple investors."

The Disciple Investing Apostle

Paul's Ministry of Relationships

Rod Culbertson

FOREWORD BY
Mantle Aaron Nance

WIPF & STOCK · Eugene, Oregon

THE DISCIPLE INVESTING APOSTLE
Paul's Ministry of Relationships

Changed Lives Changing Lives Series 2

Copyright © 2018 Rod Culbertson. All rights reserved. Except for brief quotations in critical publications or reviews, no part of this book may be reproduced in any manner without prior written permission from the publisher. Write: Permissions, Wipf and Stock Publishers, 199 W. 8th Ave., Suite 3, Eugene, OR 97401.

Wipf & Stock
An Imprint of Wipf and Stock Publishers
199 W. 8th Ave., Suite 3
Eugene, OR 97401

www.wipfandstock.com

PAPERBACK ISBN: 978-1-5326-4215-9
HARDCOVER ISBN: 978-1-5326-4216-6
EBOOK ISBN: 978-1-5326-4217-3

Unless otherwise indicated, all Scripture quotations are from The Holy Bible, English Standard Version® (ESV®), copyright © 2001 by Crossway, a publishing ministry of Good News Publishers. Used by permission. All rights reserved.

Manufactured in the U.S.A.

With gratitude to a man who invested in me through the multiple avenues of phone conversations, exhaustive teaching and training, personal hospitality, along with constant encouragement and affirmation, I dedicate this book to the Reverend Mr. Mark Lowrey, to whom, humanly speaking, I owe the foundation of my ministry philosophy and means of survival in the service of Christ and his kingdom. The founder of Reformed University Fellowship, Mark, much like the Apostle Paul, was willing to befriend me as an unknown campus minister at the University of Florida, take me under his wings from a distance, come to my aid in times of questioning and need, and to care about my progress and well-being in both ministry life and marriage, as well as in personal growth in Christ-likeness. He has been one of my valued counselors over the years while in the midst of the throes of ministry. I have admittedly taken a circuitous route to seminary teaching, but thanks to Mark's interest and investment, I have been prepared to invest in others on the seminary level. Christ is my ultimate discipler, but he has used a multitude of others who were willing to invest in me, a stumbling servant of the Gospel, and Mark is indeed one of those others. Mark's willingness to serve me and multiple other campus ministers in the past has not gone unnoticed. With many thanks, I honor him with this book.

Contents

Foreword by Mantle Aaron Nance | ix
Acknowledgements | xi
Introduction | xiii

Chapter One: Barnabas | 1
Chapter Two: Timothy | 13
Chapter Three: Silas | 18
Chapter Four: Titus | 27
Chapter Five: Tychicus | 34
Chapter Six: Epaphroditus | 37
Chapter Seven: Epaphras | 41
Chapter Eight: Trophimus | 44
Chapter Nine: Philemon and Onesimus | 47
Chapter Ten: Onesiphorus | 50
Chapter Eleven: Erastus and Aristarchus | 53
Chapter Twelve: Priscilla and Aquila | 56
Chapter Thirteen: Apollos | 59
Chapter Fourteen: Luke | 63
Chapter Fifteen: Mark | 66
Conclusion | 69

Appendix One: Paul and His Investment in "Many Others" | 71
Appendix Two: A Closer Look at Timothy and Titus | 76
Bibliography | 99

Foreword

A MINISTERIAL FRIEND AND I have sometimes joked that a standard question every aspiring minister should be asked is, "Do you love—or at least like—*people*?" While a keen interest in all species (manner) of knowledge, including theology, apologetics, biblical languages, and homiletics, is a wonderful attribute in a minister, surely an interest in and a desire to relate to one's own species should be required!

Rod Culbertson reminds us of this by examining the ministerial life of the erudite, hard charging, task-oriented Apostle Paul, who was, nonetheless, a man who loved *people*, a man whose compassion for people was a driving force behind all that he did. In Paul we find a man who did not merely have a "a mind for theology," or even a vague sort of "heart for the lost," but who rolled up his sleeves and evangelized, prayed for, encouraged, honored, discipled, rejoiced with, sorrowed over, and otherwise invested in actual *people*.

Culbertson's study opens up for us the oft-neglected yet highly impressive network of Paul's disciple-investing relationships. We learn not only from Paul but also from those in whom he invested and those who invested in him. We learn from Barnabas, Timothy, Silas, and Titus; as well as lesser-known disciples such as Tychicus, Trophimus, Erastus, and Aristarchus. We are presented with their relational dynamics—their complimentary gifts, their shared burdens and successes, their tensions, divisions, and restorations. We are reminded that God chooses to use redeemed sinners and the less-than-perfect relationships between them to build his church.

The discussion questions at the end of each chapter are carefully crafted to facilitate personal reflection and ministerial application. They help make this a profitable resource not only for individuals, but also for small group Bible studies, church staffs, and leadership teams who are looking for a biblical paradigm for investing in the lives of others with the life-transforming truths of Christ.

Ultimately, this study points to the inescapably relational nature of the Christian faith. Our God is the gloriously and eternally relational God—Father, Son, and Holy Spirit. In the gospel he has graciously chosen to restore our relationship with him, which had been lost because of our sin. And now, he has called us, who know the love of the Father, the grace of the Son, and the fellowship of the Holy Spirit, to build relationships with others that they might enter into and grow in a relationship with the God whom they were made to know. To that end, the pages that follow will challenge and equip you to follow in the footsteps of Paul and be a disciple-investor for the growth of the kingdom and the glory of our relational God.

Acknowledgements

I WISH TO ACKNOWLEDGE the late Rev. Dr. William Larkin, Presbyterian minister and long-time New Testament professor at Columbia International University, who fostered in me a greater love for both Greek and the study of the New Testament books. His ministry in my life should not go unacknowledged. I am grateful for his patient instruction and pastoral care in my life, both while in seminary, and beyond, including my labors in pastoral ministry.

A special word of thanks must also be given to my RTS Charlotte teaching assistant, Ms. Anna Unkefer, who spent countless hours editing this work and refining it for publication. She is an invaluable asset in my efforts toward publishing my books. I often wonder, "Where would I be without Anna?" Floundering, I'm sure!

Introduction

WHAT IF, SEEMINGLY EVERYWHERE you turned or every time you met someone, all you could talk about was Christ and what he has done for you? Such a scenario seems difficult to imagine. Some people, if not most, would probably think that you are either overly zealous, a religious fanatic, or just plain crazy. Accordingly, though we don't know what the Apostle Paul was doing every moment he was awake, we do find an overriding passion for the things of Christ as his constant, driving force. And his focus is not narrow—from his writings, we see that his vision is cast upon telling the *entire world* about Christ. He believes in Christ's Great Commission to go and make disciples of the nations (Matt 28:18–20) and for Paul it appears that the call to disciple making impacts his every decision, as well as his every relationship. In both Paul's letters, and in Luke's account of Paul's conversion and journeys, we observe a man who is so overcome by Christ that everyone he meets must know about God and his special Redeemer-Son, the Lord Jesus. Even while under house arrest in Philippi, we see Paul rejoicing over the "chains" that cause others to mock him—while they simultaneously proclaim Christ—knowing and being reassured that the gospel is being heard by citizens of Philippi (Phil 1:12–18). I might contend that the Apostle Paul is one of the most singularly focused individuals the world has ever known and, humanly speaking, his exuding enthusiasm and commitment is powerfully used to not only change his world but to change future world history. Paul's ministry was one of seemingly constant proclamation and teaching. Yet, the aspect of his efforts that often goes unnoticed is that his was a ministry of relationships. Paul developed numerous relationships with the people he met, taught, and served. Paul is one of the most resourceful, energetic, motivated, type "A", performance driven, strong, active, and task oriented individuals possible, but these constant energies are centered around one thing: taking the gospel to the people who need it. Relationships are an obvious theme in the life and ministry of the Apostle Paul. And these relationships were wide, diverse, and varied.

It is often implied, if not asserted, that the Apostle Paul specialized in individual discipleship and therefore set forward a model to be followed by any serious disciple maker. I do not agree with that assumption and hope to demonstrate my premise that Paul's ministry was geared toward all manner of individuals and based upon numerous methods, with relationship building being his avenue for gospel proclamation. In the realm of his relationships, I am not convinced that an intense, focused ministry to one other individual was the primary method of the Apostle. I do believe he gave Timothy extra attention and was particularly close to him as a mentor, as well as a spiritual father. However, the Apostle Paul appears to have invested himself in innumerable disciples of Jesus. In order to better understand the Apostle Paul's ministry of disciple investing, we must observe the multiple relationships he had with various individuals. He touched numerous people with his life and influence. With all due respect to the concept of individual discipleship, and hoping not to demean this vital approach to present day ministry, I believe we will observe that Paul never made his *primary* focus of ministry to be selective, personal, or individual time and attention with another. He certainly touches and impacts others in powerful, individual manners, but he also ministers in large groups, small group clusters, companionship settings, temporary outreach opportunities (evangelistic preaching), and individual miraculous healing situations.

The goal of this book is to analyze the numerous descriptions of Paul's relationships with those who might legitimately be called his fellow disciples. We will observe many references to Paul's companions, co-laborers, and friends. I will not attempt to provide a full commentary on the book of Acts or any of Paul's epistles, but hope simply to make some observations of Paul's impact on a variety of Jesus's disciples as well as their (mutual) impact upon Paul. Let's look at some of those relationships together!

1

Barnabas

Son of Encouragement

BARNABAS APPEARS TO BE one of those individuals whom everyone likes! And he is likable, unless his people orientation intrudes on the opinion of one strong-willed, driven, task-focused apostle named Paul. Although his given name is Joseph, he is known as Barnabas, since his is a ministry of encouragement or exhortation (Acts 4:36). It is possible this nickname was given to him after his conversion in Christ. Paul alludes to Barnabas's apostleship (and his singleness) in 1 Corinthians 9:4–6, "Do we not have the right to eat and drink? 5 Do we not have the right to take along a believing wife, as do the other apostles and the brothers of the Lord and Cephas? 6 Or is it only Barnabas and I who have no right to refrain from working for a living?" Barnabas first appears in the book of Acts at the time of communal sharing in the early church, immediately following the initial persecution of Peter and John for preaching Jesus at the temple. After their arrest, Peter and John are released, and the believers gather together and pray which leads to the Holy Spirit's falling upon the gathered church in power.

The spiritual revival that breaks out in the temple has happened among many diverse, out-of-towners. Their conversions have created a situation that now necessitates the sharing of personal goods for their sustenance while they dwell in Jerusalem. Barnabas, possibly a man of wealth, donates a piece of personal property, contributing the proceeds to the apostles for their use in the common pool of resources designated for the community of believers. However, rather than assuming he is wealthy, it may be that as a Levite,[1] the property may have been a gift to him in the

---

1. Hence strongly Jewish, although from Cyprus, an island of Greek and Roman

service of his ministry. Nevertheless, he certainly demonstrates his caring nature and commitment to the Lord and his people through this generous gesture. Also, as a Levite (a priestly role), we would also assume that he understands mercy, as well as the needs of others; such understanding is evident in the sacrifice of his possessions.

Diplomat and Bridge Builder

After Paul's conversion, Barnabas is the individual who boldly brings this former, life-threatening, Christian-persecuting "fireball" of a man to the disciples. Despite the fact that Paul has been preaching that Christ is both the Son of God and the Messiah in the synagogue at Damascus, he has been absent from the public eye for three years, spending what appears to be a time of study and reflection in the desert of Arabia. When he reappears and decides to go to Jerusalem to explain the changes in both his life and thinking, fearful memories of his previous persecution prevail among the believers there. Luke explains,

> And when he [Paul] had come to Jerusalem, he attempted to join the disciples. And they were all afraid of him, for they did not believe that he was a disciple. [27] But Barnabas took him and brought him to the apostles and declared to them how on the road he had seen the Lord, who spoke to him, and how at Damascus he had preached boldly in the name of Jesus. (Acts 9:26, 27)

In beautiful fashion, Barnabas becomes the diplomat, the mediator, the liaison between the church at Jerusalem, and the feared, former persecutor of the church at large. Barnabas is a well-respected, well known member of the early leadership in the church. His reputation and capacity for ministry is a tremendous asset to Paul in the infant days of his conversion, beginning with his intervention on behalf of a trembling church at Jerusalem.

Pastor/Evangelist

In Acts 11, Barnabas surfaces again and the testimony of this narrative does nothing but prove the valuable asset this committed disciple is to the church. Luke describes the origin of the first Gentile congregation and how Barnabas is involved in visionary ministry to these new believers,

---

inhabitants.

> ¹⁹ Now those who were scattered because of the persecution that arose over Stephen traveled as far as Phoenicia and Cyprus and Antioch, speaking the word to no one except Jews. ²⁰ But there were some of them, men of Cyprus and Cyrene, who on coming to Antioch spoke to the Hellenists also, preaching the Lord Jesus. ²¹ And the hand of the Lord was with them, and a great number who believed turned to the Lord. ²² The report of this came to the ears of the church in Jerusalem, and they sent Barnabas to Antioch. ²³ When he came and saw the grace of God, he was glad, and he exhorted them all to remain faithful to the Lord with steadfast purpose, ²⁴ for he was a good man, full of the Holy Spirit and of faith. And a great many people were added to the Lord. ²⁵ So Barnabas went to Tarsus to look for Saul, ²⁶ and when he had found him, he brought him to Antioch. For a whole year they met with the church and taught a great many people. And in Antioch the disciples were first called Christians. (Acts 11:19–26)

Luke tells us that the Jerusalem church sent Barnabas to view the Lord's blessing on this new church growing in unchartered waters. Barnabas is the perfect man to go—he cares about people and will be a source of inspiration to this seedling congregation. The trip is 300 miles by land but Barnabas goes. In descriptive terms Luke explains that when he arrives, Barnabas is very positive about what the Lord is doing in Antioch. God is obviously at work! Barnabas is happy to experience the Lord's activity and as is natural for him, he speaks words of encouragement for these believers to remain true to the Lord with all their hearts. Surely he brings inspiration to the members of the church because Luke expresses that Barnabas displays a "hat trick" or triad of positive elements: goodness, filling of the Holy Spirit, and fullness of faith. The result is that many more are brought to the Lord. Barnabas appears to be a natural pastor, but his ministry also bears the fruit of an evangelist.

Focused on Others

What does the above passage expose about Barnabas's relationship to Paul? He is Paul's mediator of a different sort with this group of new Christians. Barnabas's response to what God is doing in Antioch is that he travels the 120 miles required to find Saul in his home town of Tarsus (apparently Paul has been living there for a year or two). Scholars believe that Tarsus was situated on a trade route to Antioch and that route was most probably

Barnabas's course of travel. When Barnabas discovers Paul's location, he goes, finds him, and convinces him to come to Antioch. Here we observe the Son of Encouragement encouraging a church of new believers and then encouraging a highly qualified Christ enthusiast named Paul to make his next destination the city of Antioch. In some ways, it appears that Barnabas is always thinking of others. One must wonder how his vision and personality impacted the Apostle Paul in those early years of ministry.

In Acts 12, we read of Herod Agrippa's persecution in Jerusalem, the killing of James (the brother of John), and the incarceration of Peter in prison, where he miraculously escapes. Herod then leaves Jerusalem and dies in Caesarea, allowing the church to continue to grow. At this time, Luke tells us that Paul and Barnabas have returned from their mission—an apparent reference to the delivery of a gift from Antioch to the suffering and impoverished church in Jerusalem (Acts 11:30). These two men are most certainly a team and are effectively serving together. However, the text informs us that a third member has been added to the team in the person of John Mark, Mary's son and Barnabas's cousin (Acts 12:12; Col 4:10). Barnabas's natural inclination to be inclusive (so it appears) has won Paul over. The group invites John Mark to return to Antioch.

Willing to Fade

In Acts 13, Luke provides a list of prophets and teachers in the church at Antioch; Barnabas is named first, lending credibility to his leadership status and importance to the congregation of believers there. Then Luke explains,

> While they were worshiping the Lord and fasting, the Holy Spirit said, 'Set apart for me Barnabas and Saul for the work to which I have called them.' ³ Then after fasting and praying they laid their hands on them and sent them off. (Acts 13:2–3)

The first Gentile missionaries are appointed by the Holy Spirit, then confirmed through the process of fasting and prayer, and are finally commissioned by the body of Christ in Antioch to pursue the path of gospel proclamation. It is on this first missionary trip that Paul arises to exceptional prominence. At Cyprus, Paul and Barnabas, being the apparent leaders, both ("they") proclaim the gospel to the Jewish synagogues. John Mark is mentioned simply as "their helper" (Acts 13:5). Although Paul has

Barnabas and the young John Mark with him, Luke records the description of their presence as merely "Paul and his companions" (Acts 13:13).

Paul is beginning to take center stage, while John Mark, without a Lucan explanation, appears to get cold feet on the journey, leaves the traveling party, and returns to Jerusalem. F.F. Bruce surmises,

> Why John Mark left Barnabas and Paul at Perga and returned to Jerusalem is uncertain; Paul, at any rate, regarded his departure as desertion (Acts 15:38). Perhaps he did not care for the increasing rigours which evangelization in Asia Minor would involve; perhaps he resented the way in which his cousin Barnabas was falling into second place. (When the expedition sets out from Cyprus, the order is "Barnabas and Saul"; by the time they leave Cyprus, it is "Paul and his company"!) But Barnabas does not seem to have resented this at all: his greatness of soul illustrates the old couplet—
> 'It takes more grace than I can tell to play the second fiddle well.'[2]

In Pisidian, Antioch, Paul appears to perform the majority of the synagogue preaching; Barnabas is not involved. He is apparently fading into the background. However, afterward, due to a positive response by those listening, both men are invited to return the next Sabbath, and some are interested enough to engage in conversation with both of them. Additionally, Luke adds that both talk with the people and urge them to continue in the grace of God.

Gospel Vision

At this point, jealous Jews create a scene and treat Paul and Barnabas harshly, heaping abuse on them. Paul and Barnabas, in the presence of a mixed audience, both Jew and Greek, make a landmark and historic declaration: although they have brought the message of the gospel to the Jews first, they are now going to the Gentiles. They buttress their assertion by quoting Isaiah 49:6, "I have made you a light for the Gentiles, that you may bring salvation to the ends of the earth" (Acts 13:47). Those Gentiles who hear this declaration and are appointed for eternal life, believe. Luke describes how the gospel grows hand-in-hand with persecution and explains the result of these conversions:

---

2. Bruce, *Acts*, 266.

⁴⁹ And the word of the Lord was spreading throughout the whole region. ⁵⁰ But the Jews incited the devout women of high standing and the leading men of the city, stirred up persecution against Paul and Barnabas, and drove them out of their district. ⁵¹ But they shook off the dust from their feet against them and went to Iconium. ⁵² And the disciples were filled with joy and with the Holy Spirit. (Acts 13:49–52)

Together, Paul and Barnabas are able to declare the gospel to the Jew and also to the Greek in the city of Pisidian, Antioch, and to see the first glimpse of God's promise that the nations will hear of his glorious wonders and ultimately glorify him. Amidst persecution and rejection, I'm sure they reveled in the wonder of seeing God working in the world! Little did they know what was yet to come!

Bold in the Midst of Opposition

In Acts 14, this ministry of "world" (Jew and Gentile) proclamation continues as Paul and Barnabas arrive in the city of Iconium. Luke conveys what happens there:

> ¹ Now at Iconium they entered together into the Jewish synagogue and spoke in such a way that a great number of both Jews and Greeks believed. ² But the unbelieving Jews stirred up the Gentiles and poisoned their minds against the brothers. ³ So they remained for a long time, speaking boldly for the Lord, who bore witness to the word of his grace, granting signs and wonders to be done by their hands. ⁴ But the people of the city were divided; some sided with the Jews and some with the apostles. ⁵ When an attempt was made by both Gentiles and Jews, with their rulers, to mistreat them and to stone them, ⁶ they learned of it and fled to Lystra and Derbe, cities of Lycaonia, and to the surrounding country, ⁷ and there they continued to preach the gospel. (Acts 14:1–7)

This visit is, as Yogi Berra once said, "Déjà vu all over again!" Their gospel proclamation was so effective that both Jews and Gentiles believe. Yet persecution, even the threat to their lives, abounds. God is affirming his promise to declare his glory to the nations; the church, made up of both Jews and Gentiles, is being built. Nevertheless, opposition abounds. But Luke recounts how Paul and Barnabas remain in the city of Iconium and speak boldly for the Lord. The Lord, affirming their apostolic authority, confirms their message with both signs and wonders. However, the cold reception by both unbelieving Jews and Gentiles leads to rejection and a plot to harm these two men. Together they flee (most likely for their lives) and move on to the next potential field of harvest.

Paul and Barnabas then arrive in Lystra and upon healing a lame man, the superstitious crowd goes berserk, exclaiming that both men are Greek gods and believing that the city has received a special visit from the gods. To understand the substantial presence emanating from Barnabas, we see the crowds give him the name Zeus. Paul is given a rather secondary nickname, that of Hermes, who was the son of Zeus and a herald of the gods. F. F. Bruce sheds some light on this matter:

> Zeus was the chief god in the Greek pantheon; Hermes, son of Zeus by Maia, was the herald of the gods. Barnabas may have been identified with Zeus because of his more dignified bearing; Paul, the more animated of the two, was called Hermes 'because he was the chief speaker . . .'[3]

Paul and Barnabas deny these false proclamations, surely recognizing the idolatrous worship involved. But fickle crowd that they are, the Lystrans with the help of some Jews who have come from Antioch and Iconium, win the crowd over, stone Paul, and drag him outside the city, believing him to be dead. We can only assume that they attack Paul because he is the primary spokesman of the two: kill the voice and the message dies. Luke does not describe the impact that this potential loss of leadership and friendship has upon Barnabas but we can imagine that in many ways he was shocked. Nevertheless, in near miraculous fashion Paul arises and returns to the city, apparently later that same day. Barnabas must have gained a great sense of relief as well, having his own soul encouraged by the Lord in the midst of these shattering circumstances.

From Lystra, Luke documents their next trip,

> [20] But when the disciples gathered about him, he rose up and entered the city, and on the next day he went on with Barnabas to Derbe. [21] When they had preached the gospel to that city and had made many disciples, they returned to Lystra and to Iconium and to Antioch, [22] strengthening the souls of the disciples, encouraging them to continue in the faith, and saying that through many tribulations we must enter the kingdom of God. [23] And when they had appointed elders for them in every church, with prayer and

---

3. Ibid., 292.

fasting they committed them to the Lord in whom they had believed. (Acts 14:20–23)

Together, a beleaguered Paul and the Son of Encouragement continue to preach, see new disciples converted, and revisit previously evangelized cities. There, they strengthen and encourage all those believers to remain true to the faith. They convey one of the most poignant statements about their ministry, as well as the Christian life, when they conclude, "We must go through many hardships to enter the kingdom of God." The impact of these words upon their listeners must have been tremendous, considering that Paul stood in their midst, bruised and marred, broken and suffering, and "bearing on his body the marks of Jesus"! (Gal 6:17). With apostolic authority, they appoint (or oversee the election of) elders in each of these young churches, and with prayer and fasting commit them to the Lord. From there, they travel to Antioch where they report the successes and trials of their first ever missionary adventure! Of particular note is the wonderful reception of the Gentiles to the gospel. Paul and Barnabas stay in Antioch for a good while, possibly in order for Paul to recover from his physical beating and the arduous demands of the trip.

People Pleaser?

We gain further insight into the relationship of Paul and Barnabas as we consider Paul's remarks in Galatians 2:1–13, although the chronological order of these words is difficult to determine. I submit that in the Galatians passage, Paul speaks of an occurrence not recorded by Luke in the book of Acts, an occurrence that took place prior to the Jerusalem Council (below). Paul writes,

> [11] But when Cephas came to Antioch, I opposed him to his face, because he stood condemned. [12] For before certain men came from James, he was eating with the Gentiles; but when they came he drew back and separated himself, fearing the circumcision party. [13] And the rest of the Jews acted hypocritically along with him, so that even Barnabas was led astray by their hypocrisy. (Gal 2:11–13)

Some of James's brothers from his Jerusalem church had arrived in Antioch and brought their Judaizing and legalistic influences with them. Peter caves under the pressure of these heavy-handed circumcision pushers.

In response, Paul blatantly explains that Peter's failure and hypocrisy is so great that even Barnabas is led astray. Most probably Paul means that Barnabas also viewed these newly converted Gentiles to be second class kingdom citizens. Here we observe a sad story, chronologically correct or not, as Barnabas, a herald of the gospel to the Gentiles, yields to relational pressure from high profile converted Pharisees. Barnabas, ever the people person, chooses people pleasing (or group conformity) over personal conviction. Is he too soft and tender-hearted? We're not sure, but this incident could trigger a later conflict event between the two men. We are left to wonder: does Paul lose respect for the Son of Encouragement because of this particular incident?

Spiritual Leader

In Acts 15 (approximately AD 49–50), Luke explains that the first big church-wide controversy comes to a head due to the concerns that Jewish believers held over the inclusion of newly converted Gentile believers. Some leaders in Judea had made a concerted effort to travel to Antioch to teach these believers that unless they are circumcised, according to the custom taught by Moses, they cannot be saved. Being present in Antioch, Paul and Barnabas debate these couriers on the spot (Acts 15:2). Out of necessity Paul and Barnabas are appointed, along with some other believers, to go up to Jerusalem to see the apostles and elders concerning this issue. However, while reporting on the reception of the gospel by the Gentiles, their report is met by some Pharisee converts who adamantly declare, "It is necessary to circumcise them [the Gentiles] and to order them to keep the Law of Moses" (Acts 15:5). As the apostles and elders meet to discuss this question, in somewhat characteristic fashion, Peter stands up and explains his own personal liberation from Gentile prejudice, acceptance of grace for all mankind, and God's plan for inclusion of the Gentile nations. Peter concludes,

> [19] Therefore my judgment is that we should not trouble those of the Gentiles who turn to God, [20] but should write to them to abstain from the things polluted by idols, and from sexual immorality, and from what has been strangled, and from blood. [21] For from ancient generations Moses has had in every city those who proclaim him, for he is read every Sabbath in the synagogues. (Acts 15:19–21)

Based on the assembly's decision, Luke relays that "Then it seemed good to the apostles and the elders, with the whole church, to choose men from among them and send them to Antioch with Paul and Barnabas. They sent Judas called Barsabbas, and Silas, leading men among the brothers" (Acts 15:22). All four men traveled to Antioch to convey the assembly's decision to the church; after some time there, Judas and Silas returned to Jerusalem while Paul and Barnabas remained in Antioch teaching and preaching God's Word. This duo exhibits both parity (equality) and strong team work as well as unity. However, when Paul expresses the desire to return to see the churches they had previously planted, these two stalwarts of the faith have a falling out over Barnabas's nephew, Mark, whom Paul will not take.[4] The disagreement is so sharp and provocative that these two unified servants part ways; Barnabas and Mark go to Cyprus, while Paul and Silas go through Syria and Cilicia. So ends a beautiful, mutualistic relationship that had encompassed the sharing of multiple joys, hardships, set-backs, and victories together.

Observations

Barnabas begins his visible ministry by giving away one of his possessions (property) to the church's community fund at Jerusalem. He is a man with heart and a man of unity, one who sees the sacrifices necessary to benefit the greater good of others—in this case, the newly founded church. He is also a bridge-builder who ministers to Paul by becoming his public relations connection to a frightened constituency, i.e., the Jerusalem church. He increases Paul's effectiveness in ministry, endorsing him and taking the initiative towards enhancing his platform for future ministry. In the mildest sense of the word, he is a promoter of the people, hence the nickname "Son of Encouragement." In the beginning of Paul's ministry, and their relationship, Barnabas is an encouragement to both Paul and the early church. When the church at Antioch begins and Barnabas is sent there, Luke tells us that he encouraged and strengthened the believers, while also preaching with such effect that many others believed the gospel. The benefits of his ministry are evident. He once again sees the need for more aid in Antioch and accordingly makes haste to bring Paul south from Tarsus so that he may minister there. Barnabas appears to have lived by John the Baptist's creed, "He must increase and I must decrease" (cf. John 3:30), knowing that

---

4. Paul most probably viewed John Mark as a deserter on the first missionary journey.

Paul has been dramatically called and converted to preach the gospel and that if Paul's ministry increases, Christ will be lifted up.

Barnabas is committed to teamwork and we see him and Paul effortlessly working together as a team. We also see Barnabas's relational inclusivity as he invites his nephew, John Mark, to join him and Paul in their ministry efforts. Although this mild form of nepotism will cost him later, he evidently wants to profit from Mark's presence and efforts, as well as helping to assist in Mark's growth, enabling him to see the great things that God is doing. In Antioch, Barnabas is without question a key player and leader. His leadership never wanes but his willingness to allow Paul's leadership to flourish is one of the great unsung stories of the New Testament. Barnabas effectively maintains leadership and preaching roles but is slowly trumped by the great apostle, yet without an apparent complaint on his part. His belief in Mark's potential does lead to an apparent and bitter conflict with Paul. Yet, in something of a symbiotic fashion, both men benefit from their mutually shared personalities, gifts, and ministries. But in the end, their philosophical views of ministry and personal styles cause a rift between them that previous ministry experiences together cannot overcome. I believe that both men benefitted through each other's constant support, personal presence, team teaching and preaching, as well as evangelistic fervor. I believe that each engaged in disciple investing in one another's life to the benefit of God's kingdom and to his glory, faults notwithstanding.

Questions for Discussion

1. Who is the most encouraging person you have ever known (parent, teacher, coach, friend, relative, other)? How did they express or demonstrate their encouragement of others? How did they encourage you personally?

2. How does the gift or art of diplomacy help the body of Christ? When diplomacy is missing from the church, what are some results? Name some relational situations in which diplomacy is needed among believers.

3. What prevents us from being willing to let others receive the more important positions? How do we learn to "fade" into the background as others grow into more prominent spiritual leadership positions?

4. What are some examples of spiritual opposition facing Christians in the world today? How do we exhibit the "boldness of Barnabas" and find strength in the midst of persecution and resistance to our gospel convictions?

5. What are some situations that cause us to feel pressure to become "people pleasers"? How do we overcome this desire to please others first, while making the Lord second?

2

Timothy

Timothy in the Book of Acts

THE MOST OBVIOUS RELATIONSHIP in the life of Paul's ministry is a young man known as Timothy. In Acts 16:1–5 we find that Paul travels though Derbe and ends up in Lystra where Timothy lives. His mother was Jewish and what would have been called an Old Testament believer. By all appearances his father, who was a Greek, was not a believer. It is unknown whether or not Timothy was raised as a Jew or as a pagan,[1] especially since he had not undergone the Jewish rite of circumcision. But Timothy apparently had been taught the Scriptures as a child by his mother and grandmother (2 Tim 1:5).[2] It appears that when these two women believe in Christ (likely during Paul's first missionary journey to Lystra—cf. Acts 14:8–20), Timothy soon follows in their path. Before long, he has made considerable progress in his growth. Hendriksen states, "In all probability Paul, on his first missionary journey (about AD 47), had been the means of Timothy's conversion, so that from that day on he could be referred to as Paul's (spiritual) 'child' (1 Cor 4:17; 1 Tim 1:2; 2 Tim 1:2)."[3]

Sacrificial Obedience

As a young man of character, Timothy had a strong reputation among believers both in Lystra and Iconium. Thus Paul considers this young man, though inexperienced, to be an asset to both his work and his travels.

---

1. Jews would often marry into dominant Gentile families.
2. Ramsey, *Bearing*, 357.
3. Hendriksen, *Pastoral*, 34.

However, since Timothy has a Greek father, he has not yet been circumcised and the Jews in the region are watching. Undergoing this act of circumcision alone indicates the willingness of Timothy to be mentored or influenced by the "commanding" nature of the great Apostle. Timothy is willing to sacrifice himself in a literal fashion in order to be a part of this apostolic band of missionaries. Surely the influence of the senior apostle is evident in Timothy's act of obedience. The impact on Paul and Timothy's exchange on this crucial issue is apparent. Consequently, Timothy becomes an incorporated member of Paul's second missionary journey.

Trustworthy

Next, in Acts 17:14–15, we see Paul leaving Timothy (in addition to Silas) with the believers of Berea who are "eager to learn and study the Scriptures." Upon learning that aggressive agitators have come from Thessalonica to bother him, Paul wisely leaves Berea (apparently sent away by the community) but leaves Silas (designated as the primary and trusted leader) and Timothy with this new fellowship of believers. Based upon the last verse describing Paul's final hours with the new church in Philippi (Acts 16:40), Paul most probably leaves Silas and Timothy behind to encourage and/or organize this new church. Minimally, we see that Paul trusts Timothy to be a positive influence upon new believers in a setting in which he himself will be absent. Timothy's reputation (noted in Acts 16) bodes him well as a responsible "fledgling" pastor of new believers. Timothy has quickly gained both the vision and the gospel responsibility maintained by his elder mentor.

Timothy then appears in Acts 18:5, along with Silas, both having returned from Macedonia (Thessalonica). According to New Testament scholar F.F. Bruce, Paul, upon hearing their good report on the health, well-being, and steadfastness of the church at Thessalonica, is relieved of some of his concerns for them.[4] He also receives the monetary gift they bring from Philippi (2 Cor 11:8; Phil 4:15), and is thus similarly relieved (for the time being, at least) of the need to support himself through tent making. He therefore gains greater zeal and increased time for the ministry of preaching in the Jewish community in Corinth, difficult soil indeed. Timothy's faithfulness and personal effort to relay good news demonstrates the ability of the younger (in faith and age) disciple to minister to the older.

---

4. Bruce, *Acts*, 370–71.

This instance demonstrates the growing maturity and trustworthiness of Timothy, sealing him as a man with a place in the heart of the hardworking apostle.

Proven and Proving

In Acts 19, the Apostle Paul is situated in the city of Ephesus where he has experienced a lengthy (two and a half years) as well as receptive and fruitful ministry; this has been accompanied by various extraordinary miracles and even a public exorcism. Bruce suggests that Ephesus is a headquarters of sorts for the Apostle.[5] Nearing the end of this ministry of long duration—and in preparation for further travels—Paul appears compelled to send two of his most trusted men to Macedonia, as he himself again stays behind. In this incident, however, Timothy is accompanied by Erastus, rather than Silas, indicating that Timothy has been proven valuable to Paul in his ministry. Most probably, this trip is what Paul refers to in his letter to the Philippians (2:19) where he writes, "I hope in the Lord Jesus to send Timothy to you soon, so that I too may be cheered by news of you" (more on this passage below). In some ways, one might conclude that Paul's confidence in Timothy's pastoral skills is growing, and that at some point Paul may be able to fully entrust to Timothy the duties of a pastoral charge. It certainly appears that Timothy has become Paul's most trusted and appreciated right-hand man. Sadly, after Timothy and Erastus leave for Macedonia, a riot breaks out in Ephesus over the shrine of Artemis. This uproar is caused by the fear of those who anticipate a loss in their idol trade since Paul has been teaching that only one true God exists thereby making all other gods false. The exponential effect of numerous converts and the loss of idol-followers creates an undue commotion among the citizens of Ephesus. Despite the fact that Timothy has departed, Luke tells the reader that ". . . when Paul wished to go in among the crowd [to speak, clarify or calm down the masses], the disciples would not let him" (Acts 19:30). We are not sure who these disciples are, but they are convincing and influential enough to talk Paul out of his assertive intention.

---

5. Ibid., 393.

Ready Companion

Soon afterward, as recorded in Acts 20, we see that Paul gathers together the disciples in Ephesus (people with whom he had evidently become close), encourages them, and then travels on to Greece where he stays for three months. Bruce submits that these three months are the winter months of AD 56–57 and that Paul spends most of this time in Corinth where he labors in writing the epistle to the Romans, "preparing the church of the imperial capital for the visit which he hoped to pay to their city quite soon."[6] However, upon hearing about a plot against him by the Jews, he backtracks through Macedonia. He finally reaches Macedonia having been joined by a number of his companion followers in Christ, including Timothy (20:4). These companions are Gentile believers who will accompany Paul on his trip to Jerusalem. They represent the growing church of Macedonia, comprised of churches that are contributing to the needs of the impoverished church in Jerusalem. They travel ahead to Troas and wait upon the arrival of Paul and Luke (and possibly Luke's apparent brother, Titus). In Troas, the missionary band reunites and on the first day of the week, these believers gather together, break bread, and listen as Paul preaches a very lengthy sermon. As regards Timothy in this chapter, he does not stand out particularly; he is simply one of a number of other disciples of Christ and friends of Paul.

OBSERVATIONS

Timothy probably was converted under Paul's preaching, although the soil of his soul was prepared by both his mother and his grandmother. They had taught him the Scriptures as a young child and their investment in his life was a significant means toward his reception of the gospel. Little did they know that God would send an appointed man to proclaim Christ, the fulfillment of the Old Testament Scriptures. Timothy is a young man of character with a good reputation, yet his disposition is not hearty. Some who have studied him through the writings of Paul have labeled him with the nickname "Timid Timothy." His compliant disposition appears to enhance his willingness to conform to the Apostle Paul's request to be circumcised in the interest of the Jews, truly a sacrifice on his part for the sake of the gospel. Through both time and experience, Paul realizes that he can trust

---

6. Ibid., 450.

Timothy with not only the gospel but also in the role of a pastor of God's people, even if Timothy is a bit fearful. Even when Paul needs companionship, he willingly sends Timothy away to do ministry. Over time, Paul has invested in this young man and as he passes from the scene—writing in 2 Timothy—he exhorts him to be a faithful pastor of his flock.

Questions for Discussion

1. Timothy's sacrificial attitude is demonstrated in his willingness to be circumcised for the sake of the Jews whom Paul is trying to reach with the gospel (Acts 16). In what ways might the Lord call us to make sacrifices for the sake of his kingdom today?

2. Some have said that trust is the quality missing most in our relationships today. What keeps us from trusting another person? How do we build trust based relationships? How do we become trustworthy? How does Christ make a difference in our trustworthiness?

3. How does being "proven" impact trustworthiness?

4. How does frequent companionship affect trust?

3

Silas

A Leader Who Defers

SILAS (ALSO KNOWN AS Silvanus) is one of the leaders of the believers who meet together in Jerusalem over the discussion concerning the incorporation of the Gentiles into the church (Acts 15:22). Silas is selected, along with Judas (Barsabbas), to accompany Barnabas and Paul to Antioch in order to transport a letter delineating the decisions made by the leaders at the council of Jerusalem. The first two men will confirm verbally that the discussions and decisions are accurate (Acts 15:27). Silas, as a leader, is apparently more prominent than Paul at this point in time, as is Barnabas. These four companions travel the approximate distance of 300 miles from Jerusalem to Antioch. Nothing is recorded about the nature of the trip so we can only imagine the ensuing conversations, Christian fellowship, and prayer together. However, when they arrive and convey the message of the letter from Jerusalem, the people of Antioch read it, while receiving Silas and Judas (Barsabbas) as the primary spokesmen. As noted prophets (or "full of the Holy Spirit") themselves, they both encourage and strengthen the believers in Antioch (Acts 15:30–32). While some manuscripts state that afterward Silas remains in Antioch (Acts 15:34), we are uncertain about this. However, when Paul becomes eager to return to the previously visited cities from his first missionary journey, Luke tells Theophilus, the reader,

> ³⁶ And after some days Paul said to Barnabas, "Let us return and visit the brothers in every city where we proclaimed the word of the Lord, and see how they are." ³⁷ Now Barnabas wanted to take with them John called Mark. ³⁸ But Paul thought best not to take with them one who had withdrawn from them in Pamphylia and

had not gone with them to the work. ³⁹ And there arose a sharp disagreement, so that they separated from each other. Barnabas took Mark with him and sailed away to Cyprus, ⁴⁰ but Paul chose Silas and departed, having been commended by the brothers to the grace of the Lord. ⁴¹ And he went through Syria and Cilicia, strengthening the churches. (Acts 15:36–41)

We see in this passage that a shift in Paul's missionary companions occurs and that the change is significant. We see Paul's conflict management and decisiveness come into play as well, whether for good or for bad. He argues with Barnabas, jettisons the apparently fragile and undependable younger Mark, and parts company with Barnabas, a decision that must have been painful for both of them. It would appear that Paul has come to know Silas well enough and has evaluated him to the degree that he wisely chooses Silas as his traveling companion and friend in the gospel. No matter how this unpleasant scene winds up, Luke is clear that the local believers support Paul's decision by commending him (and Silas) to the grace of the Lord. Off they go.

We are left without an answer to the question, "Who was the preeminent disciple of this apostolic duo?" Noting the initiative of Paul, his previous missionary travels and experience, and the leadership he takes in choosing his team partner, one has to wonder if Paul is now "the disciple investor" of the two men. He certainly begins to take much prominence at this stage in the history of the initial missionary endeavors in the book of Acts. Luke himself writes, speaking of Paul, "*He* went through Syria and Cilicia, strengthening the churches." What else will we learn about Silas and the disciple-investing relationship of these two men?

In Acts 16:1–3, Luke records that Paul (and Silas, implied by Luke) travel through Derbe and then Lystra where Paul decides to invite Timothy to join them in their travels. This group of men (Paul, Silas, and Timothy, at least) are called "Paul and his companions" in Acts 16:6, signifying Paul's prominence (from Luke's vantage point) at this stage in time. These men are further called "they" in Acts 16:7–8. Subsequently, Paul receives the vision from the man from Macedonia, leading them into Europe for the first time. Paul's leadership, his calling from the Lord, his apostolic vision, and his Lucan prominence in the text demonstrate that Paul has now become the predominant leader, not only in this small group, but eventually in the life of the fledgling church in its entirety.

Team Sufferer

This group of itinerate missionaries travels to Philippi, a Roman colony and the leading city of that district in Macedonia. There, Lydia is converted and Paul casts a false spirit out of a fortune-telling slave girl. The crowd is kicked into a frenzy by the slave girl's owners due to their loss of income; the primary objects of attack are both Paul and Silas. Ultimately both of them are grabbed by the owners, taken to the authorities, and thrown into prison. Luke describes what happens at this point,

> [23] And when they had inflicted many blows upon them, they threw them into prison, ordering the jailer to keep them safely. [24] Having received this order, he put them into the inner prison and fastened their feet in the stocks. [25] About midnight Paul and Silas were praying and singing hymns to God, and the prisoners were listening to them, [26] and suddenly there was a great earthquake, so that the foundations of the prison were shaken. And immediately all the doors were opened, and everyone's bonds were unfastened. [27] When the jailer woke and saw that the prison doors were open, he drew his sword and was about to kill himself, supposing that the prisoners had escaped. [28] But Paul cried with a loud voice, "Do not harm yourself, for we are all here." [29] And the jailer called for lights and rushed in, and trembling with fear he fell down before Paul and Silas. [30] Then he brought them out and said, "Sirs, what must I do to be saved?" (Acts 16:23–30)

It is interesting to note that Paul and Silas remain the prominent members of the mission team. Both are pursued, placed in the inner (highly secured) cell, and have their feet fastened in the stocks. These men will not escape. One wonders what they thought as they experienced such harsh persecution and treatment for "saving" a sad, abused, mistreated, and hopeless slave girl. But amazingly, both are discovered praying and singing hymns to God (there was no hymnal)! Not only were they apparently rejoicing, but this duet has an audience (a captive audience I have to admit). Without warning, a violent earthquake occurs, loosening the stocks and opening the prison doors—this intrusion is an obvious miracle! As the jailor readies himself to commit suicide (he would have been put to death for the prisoners' escape in any case), Paul declares to him that no one has escaped; everyone is present. Interestingly, the jailor throws himself down at the feet of both Paul and Silas and cries out for salvation. How he understands this concept is conjecture, but either he has heard about the slave girl's proclamations concerning these men or he has heard the declarations about God that Paul and Silas were making as they sang God's praises together.

Luke records that "they" (both Paul and Silas we assume) answer the jailor. One has to wonder if these two leaders had to wrestle over who might get to share the gospel message to this lost, forlorn, desperate, pleading, and humble (and humbled) man. Together, it appears, they preach the gospel to the jailor and "speak the word to the jailor and his family." (The jailor's housing would have been inside the prison facility to provide easy access to his family members). Silas's profile still remains high in the text but it becomes evident that Paul is now the conflict manager (or escalator) and spokesman for the two as Paul tells the officers of the magistrate that he and Silas, being Roman citizens, have been treated improperly and unjustly. Eventually, they are released and both spend time ministering to and encouraging the believers in the small church being held in Lydia's home.

Following this very eventful stop in Philippi, Paul and his band of gospel journeymen arrive at the thriving city of Thessalonica. Here Paul heads directly to the synagogue and spends three Sabbaths reasoning with them from the Scriptures, explaining and proving that the Messiah had to suffer and be raised from the dead (Acts 17:3–4). As he proclaims that Jesus is the Messiah, there is a positive response: some Jews are persuaded, as are a large number of God-fearing Greeks, and quite a few prominent women. Luke tells us that these new believers join both Paul and Silas. Luke indicates that although Paul is the preacher or persuader of this synagogue evangelism, Silas is still a leader in the party.

Jealous Jews in Thessalonica pursue both leaders in the next scene, however, and Paul and Silas are subtly and quietly removed from town during the night. They then show up in Berea where they discover a sophisticated group of inquirers in the Jewish synagogue who are both eager and ambitious to search out the matters presented to them. Agitated Jews from Thessalonica somehow hear that Paul and his companions are in Berea, so they send a contingent there to make further trouble for him. Interestingly, this signifies that he is indeed the most prominent (or endangered) disciple of Jesus among the three. Paul is whisked away and escorted to the coast, where he eventually makes his way to Athens, essentially alone. Prior to leaving Berea, Paul instructs Silas and Timothy to join him as soon as possible. F.F. Bruce attempts to explain the travels of the three men from this point of divergence,

The movements of Silas and Timothy between Paul's departure from Berea and their rejoining him at Corinth (Acts 18:5) must be reconstructed from Luke's narrative along with Paul's narrative in 1 Thessalonians 3:1ff. It appears that, as instructed, they rejoined Paul in Athens (1 Thess 3:1), whence Timothy was sent back to Thessalonica (1 Thess 3:2). Silas was sent to some other place in Macedonia (Acts 18:5), perhaps to Philippi, as Ramsay suggests. Paul then went on from Athens to Corinth (Acts 18:1), and was rejoined there by Silas and Timothy on their return from Macedonia (Acts 18:5; 1 Thess 3:6).[1]

An "Upward" Mentor?

As challenging as following these travels may appear, the point I wish to make is that Paul, at this stage in his missionary career and ministry, has two "right-hand men" in Silas and Timothy. Interestingly, one might allude to the possibility that Silas is the upward (leader) mentor for Paul, or at least someone to whom he can look to as a leader (or the true right-hand man who is actually sharing some leadership with him); whereas Timothy is certainly a downward mentor, i.e., one being mentored (his left-hand man). Paul could almost be considered mildly ambidextrous in his leadership capacity and delegation potential, not a bad idea for any leader or disciple investor.

Paul is able to move forward without his two extra hands, knowing that they will definitely and dependably show up to meet him at some pre-arranged location (perhaps a synagogue on the Sabbath). He can also ably send them off to other previously visited places and churches, resting assured that they will carry a gospel-centered ministry wherever they travel. Paul is surely upheld and supported by both men and I imagine that Silas is constitutionally the stronger of the two. However, Paul believes in Timothy and knows he can count on him equally to fulfill the tasks presented to him. Silas has endured many of Paul's humiliations and most certainly appears willing to undergo whatever peril might assault this bold apostle of the faith; his courage and endurance is a sure proof of his strong faith and leadership.

In Acts 18, as presented by F.F. Bruce above, Silas and Timothy arrive in Macedonia (probably Corinth) and Paul is freed up to devote himself

1. Ibid., 347–48.

exclusively to preaching and interacting with the Jews there, declaring that Jesus is the Messiah. Those Jews who hear him speak respond negatively, opposing him and becoming abusive, leading Paul to declare with a sense of exasperation, "Your blood be on your own heads! I am innocent. From now on I will go to the Gentiles" (Acts 18:6b). This proclamation truly makes a huge impression on both Silas and Timothy. They will never forget, I'm sure, that the Jews were given their opportunity to respond to and receive their Messiah, the resurrected One. But upon their rejection of the message, this apostle actually intends to reach the truly unreached and unevangelized. I imagine they wondered where all of this missionary passion would take them and what role they might play in the future of this gospel expedition. For Timothy, we know that he later becomes a pastor to the Gentile church at Ephesus, due to Pauline appointment.

Quietly Faithful

As for Silas, somewhat sadly, from this point on, he disappears from the gospel narrative. He disappears from the book of Acts entirely, and from the New Testament narrative, with the exception of being referenced in the writing of Paul and Peter (concluding greetings, 1 Pet 5:12). In insightful fashion and with much conjecture, Richard Loesch, retired rector of St. James Episcopal Church in Livingston, Alabama, surmises that Silas, originally a leader in the group at Jerusalem (Acts 15:22), sides with the Judaizer faction in Jerusalem and cannot personally handle the mission to the Gentiles.[2] The Judaizers believed that a Gentile must be circumcised and become a Jew of sorts in order to be a "fully" accepted Christian. If Silas ever affirmed this thought (as amazing as it seems), his presence with Paul certainly would have been strained. It is noteworthy that he disappears from the narrative in the book of Acts at this point in time, although his absence is mysteriously left unexplained.

Assuming that Paul makes his decision to pursue the Gentiles around AD 50 and that he remains in Corinth at that time (where he stays for one and a half years), one must acknowledge that he does include Silas as his constant partner in the gospel in the salutations of both 1 and 2 Thessalonians. These letters are both written while Paul ministers in Corinth, around AD 50–51. He lists Silas prior to mentioning Timothy, so we might safely assume that Silas is still a key player as well as a more prominent

2. Loesch, *People*, 402.

member of the two "sidekicks", at least to the Thessalonican believers' experience. Silas must still be serving with Paul in loyal fashion at this time and has remained to labor with Paul in his prolonged teaching ministry to the ungodly in this city. This is observed when Paul reminds the Corinthian believers that he, Silas, and Timothy preached the Son of God, Jesus Christ, among them. And he states that Jesus has always been "Yes" and "Amen" and that this message was spoken to these believers by the trio of servants to the glory of God (2 Cor 1:19).

Finally, in a sense, seemingly supporting Rector Loesch's contention that Silas might have been prone to the influence of the Judaizers, Peter mentions his name at the end of his first general epistle some ten to twelve years after Paul mentions him in AD 51. Peter writes, "By Silvanus, a faithful brother as I regard him, I have written briefly to you, exhorting and declaring that this is the true grace of God. Stand firm in it." (1 Pet 5:12) It is interesting, at least, that Silas is with Peter, assists him in writing his letter (some surmise that he also assisted Paul with the literal writing down of his letters to the Thessalonians), and is commended highly by Peter. Whatever has happened between Paul and Silas, if anything, Silas is still faithfully serving the Lord over a decade later. With that reality in mind, any reader of the book of Acts should be encouraged.

Observations

Although not Paul's equal (due to Paul's significant commission to be the apostle to the Gentiles along with his extraordinary conversion and special revelation from the Lord Jesus Christ), Silas is a leader. He surfaces as a spiritual leader in Jerusalem although we know essentially nothing about how he got there. Nevertheless, he is submissive to the Jerusalem brethren who designate him (and Judas Barsabbas) to attend Paul and Barnabas on the trip to Antioch (Acts 15) after the Jerusalem council. Initially, Silas appears to be the most dominant of this group and it is stated that he is a prophet (some texts say "full of the Holy Spirit") and a spokesman, obviously leading through speaking gifts. He has the ability (or the gift) of encouragement and is used to strengthen these Gentile believers. Essentially and eventually he becomes Paul's most natural companion in gospel proclamation during the second missionary journey. When Paul and Barnabas have their falling out over Mark, Paul chooses Silas as his traveling partner, no light decision, as those who travel together know! Although Paul quickly moves into prominence as Luke writes the narrative of the book of Acts, it does appear that he leans upon the presence of Silas in a very beneficial manner.

In Philippi, they are providentially attacked, imprisoned, flogged, and shackled together for their faith. They sing hymns together while held in stocks. I personally cannot imagine either of them singing alone and the thought of two prisoners singing together in these unpleasant circumstances is actually quite stirring. Surely they needed each other at this perplexing moment! Silas's support of Paul could have easily gone the other direction, as in time his higher profile is lowered and his troubles becomes heavier. After their release, Silas continues to be a leader although it is now very apparent that Paul is the primary messenger and leader. Paul is also the leader to be most protected, as he is the one quietly sent away from Berea in the midst of more trouble. Silas appears to be a "second-in-command" leader at this point in the missionary journey, but after Paul declares that his primary purpose is now to reach the Gentiles, Silas, although present in Corinth during Paul's ministry there, disappears almost completely from the scene. We do not know what happens to him but apparently he understands the nature of ministry under high profile leaders because he surfaces more than ten years later as a faithful servant of the Lord, according to another notable church leader, the apostle Peter!

Questions for Discussion

1. Like Barnabas, Silas is described as a prominent or effective spokesperson in the early church, even though he travels alongside Paul. However, eventually, Paul takes the preeminent position. How do prominent leaders learn to become lesser leaders in God's kingdom and why is such humility necessary for the building of God's kingdom?

2. Silas's ministry to the church at Antioch is described as one that "strengthened and encouraged" this new church of Gentile believers (Acts 15:32). How are we, as believers, able to strengthen and encourage others in their walks with the Lord? Feel free to share any ways other believers have encouraged you in your faith.

3. What is unique about "Christian" encouragement as compared to other methods of encouraging people?

4. Although not as prominent as Paul, Silas remains a significant leader in Paul's missionary journeys, important enough to be thrown into

the Philippian jail with Paul. He commiserates with Paul in the ministry of the gospel. How does having another person suffer with you help you in the midst of suffering? Feel free to share any stories of how others have shared in your suffering? How were you helped or encouraged?

5. In Acts 16:25, we are told that Paul and Silas are arrested, thrown in jail, yet are praying and singing to God together while in prison! What do you think motivated them to pray and sing instead to complain and grumble? How does joy in the Lord overcome our negative circumstances and seeming disappointments?

4

Titus

A True Son

WE ARE ABOUT TO study a Pauline relationship that, surprisingly, never appears in the book of Acts by name. We might begin, therefore, by asking ourselves a few questions about Titus, "Where did this young man come from and how did he become qualified to be a pastor?" "What are his credentials such that the Apostle Paul would trust in him so much?" And "Did Paul have a disciple investing relationship with Titus?" As we research the Pauline references to Titus, however, we discover that in all probability, Titus is an early convert of Paul. He is mentioned in Galatians 2 where Paul writes,

> ¹ Then after fourteen years I went up again to Jerusalem with Barnabas, taking Titus along with me. ² I went up because of a revelation and set before them (though privately before those who seemed influential) the gospel that I proclaim among the Gentiles, in order to make sure I was not running or had not run in vain. ³ But even Titus, who was with me, was not forced to be circumcised, though he was a Greek. (Gal 2:1–3)

Here we see that Titus, who is mentioned twice in this passage, is a part of Paul's traveling core group of missionaries. In chronological terms, if Paul is referring to his trip to the Jerusalem Council held in Acts 15, Titus is with Paul around AD 49–50. If this is an earlier private meeting of Paul with the leaders of Jerusalem, the date might be around AD 46–47. Nevertheless, the mention of Titus's name signifies that he is a high profile personality in the eyes of the Galatians. He is most probably well known to the leaders in the Jerusalem church as well. In the introduction of Paul's letter to Titus,

Paul calls him "my true (genuine) son in a common faith." (Titus 1:4) Hendriksen implies that such a reference might well indicate that Titus is one of Paul's converts and also surmises that this conversion may have occurred on Paul's first missionary journey.[1] Has he been with Paul as a companion for the past 14 years? We simply do not know.

Beloved Gentile Friend

However, as a Greek, both of his parents, unlike Timothy, would have been Gentiles. He would not have been circumcised nor would that thought have entered Paul's mind. So, unlike Timothy who had a Jewish heritage on the female side of his parentage and was persuaded by Paul to be circumcised in order to avoid scrutiny or criticism by on looking Jews, Paul is unequivocally adamant that Titus will not bend to the pressure of circumcision. The thought of undergoing such a Jewish ritual was unthinkable to Paul in the argument concerning grace versus law. Titus is apparently "Exhibit A" for building Paul's case that Gentiles are able to receive grace apart from the Jewish rite of circumcision.

Hendriksen also provides a very helpful comparison between the personalities of Timothy and Titus, as well as Paul's relationship to them. He writes,

> Timothy and Titus have in common unwavering loyalty to the cause of the Gospel, willingness to be sent on difficult missions, high regard for their friend and superior, Paul. Yet, in one respect the two differ. Titus is more of a leader; Timothy is a follower. Titus is the type of man who is able to not only take orders but also to go ahead on his own accord (2 Cor 8:16–17). Timothy needs a little more prodding (2 Tim 1:6), although here the emphasis must fall on "a little" and not on "prodding." Titus is resourceful, a man of initiative in a good cause. One finds in him the aggressiveness of Paul. Timothy is cooperative, a man who shows this spirit even when such cooperation requires him to do things which run counter to his natural shyness. This is the way these two characters are exhibited in the Art Gallery of Holy Writ.[2]

Similarly, *The Pulpit Commentary* states: "The absence of Titus from the Acts is another proof of the fragmentariness of that book. It is evident that

---

1. Hendriksen, *Pastoral*, 37.
2. Ibid., 36.

he was an ardent, able, active fellow worker, and most beloved friend of the apostle (Galatians 2:1, 3; 2 Timothy 4:10; Titus 1:4; Titus 3:12). We learn most about him from this [2 Corinthians] Epistle."[3]

A Comforting Presence

Titus's name does appear nine times in Paul's second letter to the Corinthian church. In the realm of chronological references, Paul mentions Titus in 2 Corinthians (written approximately AD 56) a few times. In 2 Corinthians 2:12–13 we read, "When I came to Troas to preach the gospel of Christ, even though a door was opened for me in the Lord, [13] my spirit was not at rest because I did not find my brother Titus there. So I took leave of them and went on to Macedonia." Paul's visit to Troas occurred around AD 50 and Paul states that he experienced a disturbing encounter when he discovered that his brother in the Lord, Titus, was not in Troas when he arrived. Even with an open door and the true opportunity to preach the gospel, Paul was unsettled—where was Titus? William Hendriksen says that Paul went searching for Titus and found him in Macedonia and through finding him, the apostle also found relief.[4]

There is one thing to learn here: Paul's lack of peace of mind indicates that the two men had more than a functioning relationship in which much time had been invested. Titus was on Paul's mind because he remained in Paul's life and heart. Paul does mention in 2 Corinthians 7:5–7 that Titus had eventually found or returned to him, saying,

> [5] For even when we came into Macedonia, our bodies had no rest, but we were afflicted at every turn—fighting without and fear within. [6] But God, who comforts the downcast, comforted us by the coming of Titus, [7] and not only by his coming but also by the comfort with which he was comforted by you, as he told us of your longing, your mourning, your zeal for me, so that I rejoiced still more.

Paul describes the many difficulties he has faced on his missionary journeys, but at the right and providentially appointed time, God sent Titus to give the downcast apostle comfort. How long had Titus been absent? We are not sure. But it appears that Paul had sent Titus to Corinth in order

---

3. Spence, *II Corinthians*, 170.
4. Hendriksen, *Pastoral*, 38.

to discover how the church had handled and responded to his first letter (a letter of many rebukes) to them. Paul is comforted because Titus has returned and told the apostle that the believers in Corinth still long for him. They have expressed deep sorrow over the many rebukes he had sent their way and are as concerned for his well-being as much as he is for theirs. Paul cannot help but be encouraged, not only because Titus informs him that the sexual offender in the church who was excommunicated (causing the church much sorrow in the process) has not only repented and been restored, but also because the entire process has proved how devoted the church is to the ministry of Paul and Titus, his representative. And above those encouraging notes Paul writes,

> [13] Therefore we are comforted. And besides our own comfort, we rejoiced still more at the joy of Titus, because his spirit has been refreshed by you all. [14] For whatever boasts I made to him about you, I was not put to shame. But just as everything we said to you was true, so also our boasting before Titus has proved true. [15] And his affection for you is even greater, as he remembers the obedience of you all, how you received him with fear and trembling. [16] I rejoice, because I have complete confidence in you. (2 Cor 7:13–16)

Respectable Co-Worker

One can only imagine the thrill that came to the apostle to see a church he started respond to his apostolic authority in a matter of church purity and to know that, although he has sent them a sorrowful and painful mandate, the messenger he sent to inquire about the process was not only accepted but refreshed by their communion. Titus has grown in affection for these unsettled believers, partly due to the respect and reverence they gave him at his coming. We are able to observe that Paul himself respects and trusts the maturity of Titus enough to send him on such a difficult mission of inquiry. And it appears to the reader that Titus is a man who, although strong or tough enough to face potential opposition in a difficult setting, is emotional enough to express happiness by the positive relationships that have surfaced in his mission.

In 2 Corinthians 8 we see that one of the tasks or responsibilities with which Paul has entrusted Titus is to complete Paul's desire to gather a collection for the financially impoverished church in Jerusalem. This request is one that Paul had made probably a year earlier and one of which the

Corinthian church is fully aware (1 Cor 16:1–2). So in addition to the assignment of working through all of the challenges of a rather dysfunctional church, Titus is expected to, we might say, raise funds. As Paul writes, we are enabled to gain insight into the value Paul maintains regarding Titus:

> [16] But thanks be to God, who put into the heart of Titus the same earnest care I have for you. [17] For he not only accepted our appeal, but being himself very earnest he is going to you of his own accord. [18] With him we are sending the brother who is famous among all the churches for his preaching of the gospel. [19] And not only that, but he has been appointed by the churches to travel with us as we carry out this act of grace that is being ministered by us, for the glory of the Lord himself and to show our good will. [20] We take this course so that no one should blame us about this generous gift that is being administered by us, [21] for we aim at what is honorable not only in the Lord's sight but also in the sight of man. [22] And with them we are sending our brother whom we have often tested and found earnest in many matters, but who is now more earnest than ever because of his great confidence in you. [23] As for Titus, he is my partner and fellow worker for your benefit. And as for our brothers, they are messengers of the churches, the glory of Christ. [24] So give proof before the churches of your love and of our boasting about you to these men. (2 Cor 8:16–24)

From this lengthy passage, we discover that Titus and Paul are similarly concerned for the Corinthians; their hearts are united in the cause. Not only has Titus responded to Paul's appeal (indicating that Paul's leadership is more dominant), but Paul suggests that Titus was enthusiastically assertive in the matter. Titus is a leader and a team player. Titus's designation by the churches to go with Paul to carry the offering to Jerusalem speaks highly of his character and trustworthiness as well. Ultimately, Paul expresses his typical warmth and approval for a fellow servant when he calls Titus both his partner (one who shares or is a companion) and his co-worker. Paul doubly appreciates Titus, both relationally and as a fellow laborer together in the gospel enterprise.

As Paul begins to wrap up his second letter to the Corinthian church, he addresses his critics once more. In chapter 12, he writes, "Did I take advantage of you through any of those whom I sent to you? [18] I urged Titus to go, and sent the brother with him. Did Titus take advantage of you? Did we not act in the same spirit? Did we not take the same steps?" (2 Cor 12:17–18). Here Paul appeals to the trusted character and integrity of Titus, knowing full well that he has proven his own sincerity and pure interest by the co-worker to whom he has delegated the task of mediating his purposes. One can only know these types of dependable qualities as they spend time together in mutual disciple investing contexts.

Lastly, in 2 Timothy 4:10, as Paul winds down his final written communication (that we know of), he demonstrates that even at the end of his life, he can count on a number of people to continue the work of pastoral ministry and church extension. One of those he lists is, of course, Titus. Scholar Frank Gaebelein suggests that Titus's mission to Dalmatia is proof that his appointment in Crete has been completed, leading him to join Paul in Rome and then to be sent to Dalmatia at his request.[5] Once again, we do not know, but it is apparent that at the end of his life, Paul has in Titus, a man and leader who can continue the gospel work Paul began many years earlier.

Observations

Titus may be a convert of the Apostle Paul but even if he is not, Paul has great affection for him, calling him his true son in the faith. He is a traveling companion of Paul's and would therefore be a close associate. Obviously he is very dear to the Apostle. And although Titus is apparently "Exhibit A" for building Paul's case that Gentiles are able to receive grace apart from the Jewish rite of circumcision, he is not an object to be used, but viewed as a son of full affection. Titus means so much to Paul that when Titus appears to be missing in action, Paul initiates an all-out search in order to find him. The relief that Paul expresses is understood by any parent who has finally discovered a child who appears to have vanished for some mysterious reason (and I've been there). Titus's presence becomes a comfort for Paul at a time of personal distress and trial. If Barnabas can be called "the son of encouragement," Titus might appropriately receive the nickname "the son of comfort"! Titus appears to be a man who is constitutionally strong ("tough") while also expressing real emotions in moving settings ("tender"). Paul thinks enough of this son of the faith to appoint him to a very trying pastoral situation in Crete. Titus is a leader willing to do the dirty work of ministry and Paul has such confidence in him that he can safely delegate a difficult task to this dependable son. Paul has seen and experienced Titus's integrity, work ethic, and reliability. Disciple investing

---

5. Gaebelein, *2 Timothy*, 414.

provides a firsthand understanding of what God is doing in and through another's life and draws us so close to our disciples that they become children of a known entity of predictable quality.

Questions for Discussion

1. Titus is seen as a comforting presence to the Apostle Paul when Paul finds him in Macedonia. What are some ways that believers are able to comfort one another when they find another person in distress?

2. The Apostle Paul apparently finds relief from the assurance that Titus is safe in his presence. Obviously Paul cared for Titus and anticipated his coming for some time! I once heard marriage and family life expert, Don Meredith, ask the question, "Who thinks about you in the middle of the day? Who loves you so much that you come to their mind when the chores and daily grind of life would otherwise distract them?" So, I ask the question: Who do you love so much that you think about them or they think about you in the middle of the day and why? What does this reality say about the power of human relationships?

3. Titus is a bearer of good news about the church at Corinth (i.e., the Corinthian believers long for Paul; a disciplined sexual offender in the church has repented). When you think of your local church, what are some positive things you could say about it? What is God doing among the believers there?

4. The church at Corinth respects Titus, and Paul both respects and trusts him as well. Titus has represented Paul well! What are the attributes of a person to whom you give respect? What prevents us from respecting another person?

5

Tychicus

Valuable Brother

A LESSER KNOWN COMPANION to Paul is discovered in the person known as Tychicus, man of Asia, a true Greek. He appears suddenly in the book of Acts in chapter 20:4,

> ¹ After the uproar ceased, Paul sent for the disciples, and after encouraging them, he said farewell and departed for Macedonia. ² When he had gone through those regions and had given them much encouragement, he came to Greece. ³ There he spent three months, and when a plot was made against him by the Jews as he was about to set sail for Syria, he decided to return through Macedonia. ⁴ Sopater the Berean, son of Pyrrhus, accompanied him; and of the Thessalonians, Aristarchus and Secundus; and Gaius of Derbe, and Timothy; and the Asians, *Tychicus* and Trophimus. ⁵ These went on ahead and were waiting for us at Troas. (Acts 20: 1–5; emphasis mine)

The Apostle Paul highly values Tychicus. He describes him as his dear brother and faithful servant of the Lord in Ephesians 6:21. Tychicus also appears to be a messenger from Paul to the Ephesians. Along with Trophimus, Tychicus is a man of Asia (the Roman province of Asia, of which Ephesus is the capital). In Acts 20, we find him accompanying Paul, along with others at the tail end of Paul's third missionary journey, as he returns from Greece into Macedonia and into Asia with the purpose of going to Jerusalem with a charitable gift.[1]

---

1. Hendriksen, *Pastoral*, 321.

As he sits, imprisoned under house arrest, Paul tells the Ephesians, "So that you also may know how I am and what I am doing, Tychicus . . . will tell you everything.²² I have sent him to you for this very purpose, that you may know how we are, and that he may encourage your hearts." (Eph 6:21–22)

Dependable and Faithful

In Colossians 4:7–8, Paul also writes,

> ⁷ Tychicus will tell you all about my activities. He is a beloved brother and faithful minister and fellow servant in the Lord. ⁸ I have sent him to you for this very purpose, that you may know how we are and that he may encourage your hearts, ⁹ and with him Onesimus, our faithful and beloved brother, who is one of you. They will tell you of everything that has taken place here.

The remarks from Colossians 4 are almost the same words that Paul uses in the Ephesians 6 passage above in regard to Tychicus. He is a man sent from the side of Paul. Apparently, he is the bearer of the epistle, therefore a highly regarded courier. Obviously, Paul has a fond affection for Tychicus and wishes to build a receptive attitude in the two churches at Colossae and Ephesus based on their common spiritual heritage in Christ—he is their brother. Paul is convinced that Tychicus is a very faithful servant and minister and a willing messenger. We can assume that Tychicus's faithfulness to the Lord is one reason Paul utilizes him as his "press man" with these two churches. Paul has confidence in him. If you are concerned about Paul and want an update, ask Tychicus—that's why he's here! In addition, Paul is convinced that Tychicus's report on Paul's well-being would be an encouragement and comfort to them. Paul has held up well despite the persecution and imprisonment and that is just the message Paul wants Tychicus to convey.

In the second letter to Timothy, as Paul wraps us his final words (4:12), he mentions that he has sent Tychicus to Ephesus. As the bearer of the letter to the Ephesians during the years AD 60–61, Tychicus is a natural person to send again to the church at Ephesus as Paul sits in a Roman dungeon a few years later (AD 63–64). Paul's confidence in Tychicus's faithfulness and servanthood must be reassuring as the apostle faces his imminent death. In Titus 3:12, Paul writes Titus, pastor of the contrary church in Crete, that in order to enable or free Titus to come visit with Paul (who is going to remain immobile for the winter months), the apostle will send an interim pastor, so to speak, to relieve him in his ministry. We do not know for certain who this is, but that substitute pastor might well be Tychicus, trusted, faithful servant.

Observations

In summary, Tychicus is portrayed as a very reliable, dear brother who is truly willing to serve the Lord. Ultimately, he is willing to apply that faithful servant attitude by serving the Apostle Paul. He will travel on Paul's behalf, carry Paul's crucial correspondence, and provide pastoral ministry in an interim fashion, if needed, so that Paul can visit with a key ministry leader. Tychicus has kingdom vision and is willing to honor that vision through quiet service to the Lord's servants and to the Lord Himself. The quiet leader can be an effective leader. And the quiet believer who serves the Lord first, and others second, can be a very effective member of Christ's body, the church. Reliable servanthood, done with a willing heart and needing no public affirmation, provides effective ministry. Like Titus, the true Christian servant looks to the needs of Christ's kingdom and makes every effort to serve Christ's church. Paul and Tychicus appear to demonstrate oneness of heart, the inevitable outcome of a positive, mutual disciple investing relationship.

Questions for Discussion

1. From the descriptions and passages above, why does the Apostle Paul love and value Tychicus?

2. Tychicus is known for his faithfulness. How do you define or describe faithfulness? How is a person's faithfulness proven? Describe a person whom you have observed exhibiting faithfulness.

3. How would you teach another person to be reliable and conscientious? What Scripture passages would you use to do so?

4. Why should Christians exhibit faithfulness and reliability more than those who do not believe in Christ? What motivates a Christian to be faithful and reliable?

6

Epaphroditus

Beloved Risk Taker

EPAPHRODITUS IS MENTIONED ONLY twice in Scripture and both times the references are from the hand of Paul in the same book, his letter to the church at Philippi. Yet, in these two references, the apostle provides extensive insight into the heart of this committed believer in Christ. Apparently Paul knows him very well, although probably only briefly. The first mention of his name occurs immediately after Paul explains to the Philippian believers that as soon as he is able, he will send Timothy to check on them both as a church and in regard to their faith (2:19–24). His praise of Timothy is extraordinary as we have seen previously. However, his love and appreciation of Epaphroditus is almost as stirring as that for Timothy, his beloved son. Paul writes,

> [25] I have thought it necessary to send to you Epaphroditus my brother and fellow worker and fellow soldier, and your messenger and minister to my need, [26] for he has been longing for you all and has been distressed because you heard that he was ill. [27] Indeed he was ill, near to death. But God had mercy on him, and not only on him but on me also, lest I should have sorrow upon sorrow. [28] I am the more eager to send him, therefore, that you may rejoice at seeing him again, and that I may be less anxious. [29] So receive him in the Lord with all joy, and honor such men, [30] for he nearly died for the work of Christ, risking his life to complete what was lacking in your service to me. (Phil 2:25–30)

Epaphroditus is a member of the church at Philippi and has brought Paul a gift that the church collected for him (4:18). Yet in bringing that gift, he has risked (2:30) and apparently almost lost his own life (2:27). He falls ill either on the trip or after he arrives, having found Paul. His illness appears very serious. Interestingly, Paul does not heal him nor mention anything about a miraculous recovery, but he does recover. He simply says, "God had mercy on him, and not only on him but on me also, lest I should have sorrow upon sorrow." Now that Epaphroditus is physically able, Paul writes that he is sending him back. (He is the carrier of the letter, which is a thank-you letter of sorts, prompted by the gift.)

In these two references to Epaphroditus, the expressions Paul uses to describe him are significant. Speaking of Epaphroditus in chapter 2 of the letter, Paul says that he is . . .

1. Paul's brother, indicating the affection Paul has for him as a family member in Christ (2:25).

2. Paul's co-worker, a not-so-lightly-used phrase by the apostle who understood the nature of ministerial and missionary work in the kingdom (2:25).

3. Paul's fellow soldier, a very strong phrase expressing the nature of spiritual warfare that Paul fully understands (2:25).

4. The church at Philippi's messenger, a willing servant who was asked to transport a special gift raised by the church on his behalf (2:25).

5. The church at Philippi's messenger, who is able to convey the care of the church for the apostle who founded the church (2:25).

6. One who "longs" for the Philippian believers, demonstrating his heart for his own people and love for God's people in the church (2:26).

7. A man who has a troubled or distressed heart for his own people (2:26).

8. An honorable man because he almost died for the work of Christ (2:27, 29).

9. One willing to risk his life (2:30); we know that Paul, who risked his life a number of times, would be deeply impressed by Epaphroditus's effort on his behalf.

Epaphroditus ministers to Paul as Paul has ministered to the Philippians. Paul brought the gift of the gospel to the church at Philippi in their time of need, and the church at Philippi through Epaphroditus brought a gospel gift to Paul in his time of need. We are left with some questions about the extent of these men's personal relationship: Did Paul lead Epaphroditus to the Lord while in Philippi or did he convert later through the influence of the local church there? Had they ever met or spent time together prior to the delivery of the gift to Paul? How long was Epaphroditus ill and did Paul spend time with him in recovery? Was the risk of his life due simply to over exhaustion or ensuing illness, or was it due to the danger involved in coming to Rome to visit a man imprisoned for his faith in Christ? We can only conjecture about the answers to these questions.

Observations

With respect to these two men's relationship, we certainly observe mutual disciple investing, two believers willing to demonstrate gospel based service to one another as well as to the local church at Philippi. In many ways, although Paul is clearly the apostle being served, he elevates Epaphroditus to an equal status when he calls him a brother, a co-worker, and a fellow soldier. Paul knows him well enough to have discerned his heart's longings and his distress for his fellow believers. And I believe it is clear that Paul not only holds Epaphroditus in high regard for his life-risking trip, but that he deeply understands and respects the ministry mentality that Epaphroditus has demonstrated on his behalf.

Questions for Discussion

1. The Apostle Paul describes Epaphroditus with three descriptions: "my brother and fellow worker and fellow soldier." Compare and contrast these concepts. Which of these descriptions do you think Paul appreciated the most about Epaphroditus and why?

2. Epaphroditus is described by Paul as one who "risked his life for the work of Christ." What motivates us to sacrifice ourselves for the sake of Christ and his kingdom? In what ways can we sacrifice for Christ in our daily lives?

3. What are some of the emotions or passions displayed by Epaphroditus? What is he emotional about? Why do we tend to refrain from exhibiting emotions in such a way that others notice? What are we missing when emotions are absent from our church community and our relationships?

4. How can we develop a greater love for other believers so that we are willing to lay down our lives for them? In what simple ways can we love them or express our love to them on a daily basis?

7

Epaphras

Gospel-Oriented Churchman

EPAPHRAS IS NOT NECESSARILY a key player in the ministry and life of Paul, but Paul played a role in both his conversion and in his elevated status among his own people, the church at Colossae. Epaphras is usually understood to be a pastor among the congregation of Colossae, a church with which the apostle has no apparent direct association. From the accounts of the book of Acts, it appears that Paul did not start this church. Nevertheless, Paul preached the gospel in the region, and had a headquarters of sorts in Ephesus, where he lived for around three years. We can surmise that during this time the apostle came into contact with and was a part of Epaphras's conversion, since Epaphras was a citizen of the city of Colossae (Col 4:12). Epaphras understood the gospel and went back home and told others, thus precipitating the start of churches in the Lycus Valley, including Colossae, Laodicea (Col 4:15), and Hierapolis.

In the opening words of the epistle to the Colossians (chapter 1), Paul writes these words about Epaphras:

> ³ We always thank God, the Father of our Lord Jesus Christ, when we pray for you, ⁴ since we heard of your faith in Christ Jesus and of the love that you have for all the saints, ⁵ because of the hope laid up for you in heaven. Of this you have heard before in the word of the truth, the gospel, ⁶ which has come to you, as indeed in the whole world it is bearing fruit and increasing—as it also does among you, since the day you heard it and understood the grace of God in truth, ⁷ just as you learned it from Epaphras our beloved fellow servant. He is a faithful minister of Christ on your behalf ⁸ and has made known to us your love in the Spirit. (Col 1:3–8)

Then, in the closing words of the epistle to the Colossians (chapter 4), Paul writes these words about Epaphras:

> ¹² Epaphras, who is one of you, a servant of Christ Jesus, greets you, always struggling on your behalf in his prayers, that you may stand mature and fully assured in all the will of God. ¹³ For I bear him witness that he has worked hard for you and for those in Laodicea and in Hierapolis. ¹⁴ Luke the beloved physician greets you, as does Demas. ¹⁵ Give my greetings to the brothers at Laodicea, and to Nympha and the church in her house. (Col 4:12–15)

From these two passages we learn much about Epaphras from the perspective of Paul. He is . . .

1. An evangelist who has taught the gospel of God's grace to the people of this region and who, in turn, has seen it bear fruit and grow (3:5, 7).
2. A dear, fellow servant, a posture that means everything to the apostle Paul, engendering his respect for Epaphras (3:7).
3. A faithful minister of Christ on Paul's behalf, having visited the three cities of the Lycos Valley with the gospel as an overflow of Paul's ministry in Ephesus (3:6).
4. One of the members of the Colossian church (4:12).
5. A proven servant of Jesus Christ (4:12).
6. Not only one who prays but one who wrestles (agonizes or struggles) in prayer and petitions on the behalf of others, including the believers in the local churches there (4:12).
7. One who prays for believers to stand firm (or hold their ground) in God's will so that they might become mature and assured (4:12).
8. One who is a hard worker for the three churches in the Lycus Valley (4:13).

Finally, Epaphras appears in the letter Paul writes to Philemon, i.e., the companion letter to Colossians. Here Paul mentions him as his fellow prisoner in Christ Jesus. We might conjecture that he went to visit Paul and the persecution of Nero broke out on a more full-scale effort, landing Epaphras in prison with Paul. This would make more sense than the possibility that Epaphras is an outside visitor trying to take care of the apostle while he is in prison, although that thought could be the reality of the situation. Paul is in prison with Onesimus, slave of Philemon, so it does appear that he has at least two Christian prison companions. Paul probably appreciates Epaphras's presence with him and he mentions his gratitude to Philemon who knows Epaphras. The letter to Philemon and the letter to the church at Colossae were both probably carried by Tychicus.

Observations

To summarize, it appears that Paul led Epaphras to the Lord sometime during his stay in Ephesus. We might conjecture that since Paul lived in Ephesus for over two and a half years, he may have spent considerable time with Epaphras prior to his returning home to the Lycus Valley. One would think that they have a good relationship since Paul appears very happy about Epaphras's gospel proclamation and extols him to the church at Colossae. Paul has also seen Epaphras's intense prayer life on behalf of his own people and believes that he is truly a servant and a hard worker. These sorts of evaluations and commendations would not come from the hand of Paul without personal observation. Paul has most certainly poured into Epaphras in some manner and with great effect, considering that Epaphras is probably the pastor of the church in Colossae. No matter how it all happened, this story is a picture of disciple investing at its best.

Questions for Discussion

1. Paul twice describes Epaphras as a servant. He calls him both a "fellow servant" and a "servant of Christ Jesus." How has Epaphras served Paul and the church of Christ? Who do you know that is exemplified as a servant of God? Why is the servant's role underappreciated in the local church? How do we develop a servant attitude in ourselves and our own lives?
2. What does it mean to "struggle" on behalf of others in prayer?
3. Why is prayer "work"? And why is prayer on behalf of others even more work?
4. What motivates us to engage in intercessory prayer (prayer for others)?
5. How does the practice of prayer relate to the practice of active ministry on behalf of others?

8

Trophimus

Low-Profile Companion

TROPHIMUS, ALONG WITH TYCHICUS, appears initially in Acts 20:4. Paul is on his third missionary journey and stops in Greece where he stays three months. Luke mentions that Paul heads on to Macedonia taking a number of traveling companions with him, among whom are Trophimus and Tychicus. Luke informs the reader that both are from the providence of Asia. These men and the others actually go ahead of Paul into Troas where they wait five days for Paul and Luke to arrive. Then they remain in Troas for one week. Presumably, the reason Trophimus is with Paul is that he, among others from various churches, is accompanying the apostle on his voyage to Jerusalem. He is probably part of the contingent carrying the contributions of the churches for the impoverished believers in the Jerusalem church.

In 1 Corinthians 16, Paul writes,

> [1] Now concerning the collection for the saints: as I directed the churches of Galatia, so you also are to do. [2] On the first day of every week, each of you is to put something aside and store it up, as he may prosper, so that there will be no collecting when I come. [3] And when I arrive, I will send those whom you accredit by letter to carry your gift to Jerusalem. [4] If it seems advisable that I should go also, they will accompany me. [5] I will visit you after passing through Macedonia, for I intend to pass through Macedonia, [6] and perhaps I will stay with you or even spend the winter, so that you may help me on my journey, wherever I go. [7] For I do not want to see you now just in passing. I hope to spend some time with you, if the Lord permits. [8] But I will stay in Ephesus until Pentecost, [9] for a

wide door for effective work has opened to me, and there are many adversaries. (1 Cor 16:1–9)

From these instructions to the Corinthians, it appears that Paul has both a plan and probably a pattern to request various churches to donate money for the poor church at Jerusalem. Along with the money, Paul would like for the church to send a representative (or possibly more than one). Trophimus is apparently a representative from the church at Ephesus. In Acts 21:29 Trophimus is designated "the Ephesian" and is apparently one of Paul's Greek companions accused of being taken into (and defiling) the temple in Jerusalem. William Hendriksen says, being an Ephesian, he became the innocent cause of Paul's seizure by the mob in Jerusalem.[1] Since Paul mentions his name in 2 Timothy 4:20: "Erastus remained at Corinth, and I left Trophimus, who was ill, at Miletus," we would understand that he must have been traveling on a trip prior to Paul's Roman imprisonment and had become so ill that Paul had to leave him behind. Interestingly, we see that Paul does not heal him, but reluctantly leaves him behind.

Observations

All we can really learn about Paul and Trophimus's disciple investing relationship is that Trophimus is willing to travel with Paul as he delivers the gift to Jerusalem. He has spent a lot of time with Paul, so much so that it is noteworthy that Paul includes him in a list of people he wishes were with him during this dreadful prison experience. Paul is rather matter of fact about Trophimus's absence; yet one can hear a tone of regret that he has to leave him behind ill and is unable to benefit from his fellowship and support in a time of grave need. Disciple investing creates bonds of friendship, support, and love that are difficult to forsake. Love is often painful when the relationship is deep and abiding and then separation occurs. Parting translates into personal disappointment when mutual attachments are strong. Disciple investing creates some strong mutual attachments!

Questions for Discussion

1. If you were taking a trip to do some sort of ministry, especially a potentially dangerous trip, what type of person would you want to travel

---

1. Hendriksen, *Pastoral*, 332.

with you? In your thinking, what qualifications would you desire in them?

2. Paul takes Trophimus along with him as he transports a gift to the poor church in Jerusalem, even though as a full blooded Gentile trouble might arise with his detractors, the Jews in Jerusalem. What does this say about Paul's wisdom and judgment, as well as his selection of companions? What was Paul thinking?

3. Trophimus is never considered to be a key player in Paul's ministry, yet we see him playing a vital role in the taking of the gift to Jerusalem. We might say that Trophimus is one of the "unknown heroes" of the faith in the early church, willing to tag along and serve where needed. Who do you know that might be considered an unknown hero of the faith? Why?

4. How does separation from someone we love affect us? As believers in Christ, how do we handle this normally painful situation?

9

Philemon and Onesimus

Equals in Christ

THE LETTER TO PHILEMON is a portrait of the art of diplomacy from the hand of the Apostle Paul. Paul writes to Philemon in a letter filled with the gospel of grace to convince him to receive a man by the name of Onesimus. In this letter we see the breadth of Paul's ministry as he tries to bridge a relational gap created between slave and owner, both of whom are Christians. Onesimus is a convert of the Apostle Paul while both are imprisoned together (Phlm 1, 10). He is a runaway slave who has been captured and placed in prison. Paul writes the small letter to Philemon to lobby for proper Christian treatment for this recalcitrant slave as he is returned to his master. Paul calls Philemon a beloved brother and fellow worker, terms that the apostle does not throw around lightly (Phlm 1). Philemon is a member of the church at Colossae and it is quite possible that the church at Colossae meets in his home (Phlm 2).

Paul demonstrates his heartfelt love for Philemon with these words:

> ⁴ I thank my God always when I remember you in my prayers, ⁵ because I hear of your love and of the faith that you have toward the Lord Jesus and for all the saints, ⁶ and I pray that the sharing of your faith may become effective for the full knowledge of every good thing that is in us for the sake of Christ. ⁷ For I have derived much joy and comfort from your love, my brother, because the hearts of the saints have been refreshed through you. (Phlm 4–7)

Paul has probably never met Philemon, but has received an excellent report on him from Epaphras, the spiritual leader/pastor of the church at Colossae. Onesimus has probably conversed extensively with Paul about Philemon as well. In reality, however, through this short letter, Paul disciples Philemon as he compliments and commends him for his many Christian virtues (faith, love, and refreshment of the saints in Colossae) so that he can teach him to apply these same virtues in regard to his fugitive slave, Onesimus.

He appeals to Philemon to receive Onesimus as both his (Paul's) son in the faith (i.e., his spiritual child via his conversion and new birth; Phlm 10) and as his very heart. Paul wants Philemon to learn the greatness of the very grace he himself has received through Christ. Paul wants to instruct him about how to love the broken from the heart, willingly, and not under compulsion. Paul is teaching Philemon that because God's forgiveness is so vast, he can be the brother of a slave, even his own slave. As Paul disciples Philemon through this letter, we are able to observe the mutual ministry of disciple investing as Paul explains (verse 20) that Philemon can minister to and even refresh him while he sits in Roman shackles.

Paul's disciple investing in the life of Onesimus is evident as he writes these phrases, "(Formerly he was useless to you, but now he is indeed useful to you and to me.) [12] I am sending him back to you, sending my very heart. [13] I would have been glad to keep him with me, in order that he might serve me on your behalf during my imprisonment for the gospel" (Phlm 11–13).

Onesimus has been turned around. He had run away from Philemon but he was also running from God. A runaway slave is of no use to his master but a Christian slave is useful to both his master and to the man who leads him to a new, much greater master. As a matter of fact, Paul states that he is so useful in regard to gospel ministry that the apostle would like to retain him. Surely, he has had a glorious and genuine "prison conversion," one that is indisputable as attested to by the Apostle himself. Paul has benefitted him with the gospel and Onesimus can be of gospel benefit to his tutor in the faith. Paul, Philemon, and Onesimus—together they are a beautiful picture of a triangle of disciple investing.

Observations

One noticeable attribute of the Apostle Paul that is often overlooked is that he is able to build bridges with people from very different socio-economic backgrounds. Apparently, he has never met Philemon, but he knows exactly how to handle this Christian gentleman. He actually disciples him through the use of a well-worded letter filled with God's grace. If discipleship is investing in others and leading them to respond both to Christ and become like Christ, Paul has the ability to do so without shaking a hand or granting a hug. His affection, appreciation for, and diplomacy with Philemon is plastered all over his letter. This slave owner, bereft of a runaway slave, cannot help (we imagine) but respond to such courteous and grace-centered wooing. At the same time, Paul has obviously helped Onesimus turn his life around in such a way that he would freely choose to return to his master (slavery in the first century was frequently designed as an indentured servitude to pay off a debt to another). As a recent believer, Onesimus's life has gone from useless for Onesimus to a dual usefulness, one who could serve the master and the master disciple investor! When the disciple investor focuses upon the gospel and the benefits it provides to the life of the believer, others benefit as well. The joys of disciple investing are immeasurable.

Questions for Discussion

1. Read the letter of Philemon and note the spirit in which Paul writes. Where do you see the theme of "grace" in the letter?

2. What do you think went through Philemon's mind when he first heard that Paul was writing a letter about his runaway slave, Onesimus? How does Paul prepare Philemon for his request to receive Onesimus back into his presence?

3. What does this letter indicate about Paul's relationship with Philemon? With Onesimus?

4. What can we learn about the heart of Paul as we read this letter? How does he express his emotions?

10

Onesiphorus

Refreshing Helper

ONESIPHORUS IS ONLY MENTIONED twice by Paul, both times in his second letter to Timothy. In chapter 1 of 2 Timothy, Paul writes these words about Onesiphorus, phrases that shine like sparkling diamonds on a jeweler's black background:

> [15] You are aware that all who are in Asia turned away from me, among whom are Phygelus and Hermogenes. [16] May the Lord grant mercy to the household of Onesiphorus, for he often refreshed me and was not ashamed of my chains, [17] but when he arrived in Rome he searched for me earnestly and found me— [18] may the Lord grant him to find mercy from the Lord on that Day—and you well know all the service he rendered at Ephesus. (2 Tim 1:15–18)

The black background for the Apostle Paul is his companions' unexpected desertion of him in the province of Asia. Paul's very life is now being threatened. He is heading to trial and apparent friends and believers have abandoned him. Is fear their reason for turning back or away? Does Paul resent them? We are unsure, but the bottom line is that he has few to attend to him and comfort him while in his chains. Nevertheless, Onesiphorus brightens the forlorn apostle's life. He refreshes his spirit, not just once but in constant fashion. His presence is a lift to Paul. He does not allow the clanking chain to dissuade him from friendship and support.

As a matter of fact, he wants to be with Paul so badly that he inquires about his location and seeks him in order to be with him in his time of need. Hendriksen writes, "The words, 'and he found me' sound like an exclamation from the hand of Paul."[1] In three verses, Paul asks the Lord to grant him mercy two times, a significant act on Paul's part that demonstrates the depth of his gratitude. And then Paul reminds Timothy that Onesiphorus has been a frequent helper to his ministry while in Ephesus. Timothy has seen this servant's commitment to service.

Paul is building up Onesiphorus in the eyes of Timothy, probably as a strategy to encourage the young pastor in his own ministry as Paul prepares to depart this world. At the end of the letter (4:19), Paul once again mentions Onesiphorus, saying, "Greet Priscilla and Aquila and the household of Onesiphorus." Why mention "the household" and not just Onesiphorus himself? We simply do not know (some think that Onesiphorus has died and only his household remains). But we do know that Paul greatly appreciated this disciple's ministry in his life while he faced growing trouble. Again, another refreshing picture of mutual disciple investing!

Observations

The depth of Paul's appreciation of Onesiphorus is seen in one sentence, albeit a long one. I recently read a tribute from one friend to another, the latter suffering from lung and colon cancer, which stated, ". . . thank you for leading me to understand Jesus better through your life and example. You have been a doorway to the Door." What a profound statement. The Apostle Paul could easily summarize the ministry of Onesiphorus as "refreshing friend, unashamed faith, servant follower of Christ!" Onesiphorus fittingly displays the concept of "mutual disciple investing." Certainly he has profited from the Apostle Paul's prolific ministry; yet, in a couple of sentences, Paul demonstrates that he, himself, has profited from the love and ministry of Onesiphorus. Here is man who can refresh the persecuted, display pride in a servant suffering on behalf of the gospel, and serve in a time of need. He has aggressively pursued the imprisoned Apostle, despite his adverse circumstances. Both appear to bless each other. And if the lesser known disciple has indeed passed on in some fashion and left behind a grieving household that needs the mercy of the Lord, Paul has provided both them, and all those who read his final epistle, a proper epitaph describing the beautiful ministry that Onesiphorus has provided for him. "Refreshing—unashamed—servant!" What a grand testimony of a man who engaged in

---

1. Hendriksen, *Pastoral*, 239.

the gospel on behalf of its biggest proponent in those vital, early days of its proclamation.

Questions for Discussion

1. The Apostle Paul is undergoing a great trial in his life—he is in prison. What do you need from others when you go through a great trial in your life?

2. What are the positive contributions that others can provide when we go through trials?

3. What are some of the ways that others fail to help us when we go through trials? (Try not to become too negative on this question!)

4. What are some specific blessings or help you have seen or received from others when going through the trials of life?

5. Name someone you know who is so positive in Christ that you would love to have him/her by your side during a tough time in your life? What makes them special to you?

11

Erastus and Aristarchus

Erastus

Helpful Companion

ERASTUS IS ANOTHER COMPANION of Paul who also appears only twice in the New Testament. Yet in these two references, Erastus appears to be a very important member of Paul's traveling missionary party, at least during the third missionary journey. In Acts 19:22, he is listed as Paul's helper (approximately AD 53–54). As small as that might sound, Luke includes Timothy's name as a helper of Paul as well. While in Ephesus, Paul decides to go to Jerusalem, passing through Macedonia and Achaia on the way. He reasons, "After I have been there, I must also see Rome" (Acts 19:21b). He then sends two of his helpers, Timothy and Erastus, to Macedonia, while he stays in the province of Asia a little longer. However, Erastus is not mentioned three months later in the lengthy list of Paul's companions described in Acts 20:1–4. Nevertheless, his name *does* appear in 2 Timothy 4:20 ten years later (AD 64–66), when Paul writes that he has had to leave him in Corinth.[1] Ten years—that's a long-term relationship in a time without technology, no matter how it functioned. One might describe their relationship as "faithful friends."

---

1. We should point out that most historians do not believe he is the same Erastus (i.e., the city director of public works—or treasurer), mentioned in Romans 16:23.

THE DISCIPLE INVESTING APOSTLE

Aristarchus

Fellow Sufferer

Aristarchus is a traveling companion of the Apostle Paul, who, along with Secundus, is a Macedonian from Thessalonica (Acts 20:4; 27:2). We can assume that he became a believer during Paul's original missionary visit to Thessalonica (Acts 17:1–10). He travels with Paul on his third missionary journey and on the voyage to Rome (Acts 27:2). He is seized with Paul, along with Gaius, during the riot of the Ephesians (Acts 19:29), and after that disturbance calms down, travels with Paul and other companions on to Macedonia. Later, he becomes a fellow prisoner with Paul (Col 4:10) in his Roman (house arrest) imprisonment. It may be that Aristarchus is not an actual prisoner but his loyal presence to Paul during his imprisonment has earned him this moniker of association with Paul. He has "joined" Paul in his prison confinement.

Paul mentions Aristarchus by name and calls him a fellow worker in the two companion letters to the church at Colossae and to Philemon, letters that are written during Paul's first imprisonment. At the least, we see this fellow disciple (and most probably a convert) of Paul as one who suffers gospel persecution, joining the man who told him about Jesus. Although we do not know if Aristarchus is physically present with Paul for all of this time, he spends eight to ten years ministering alongside him in some fashion, which explains the context of attack and suffering. Paul may have led him to the Lord, but in doing so, he is ministered to by a very faithful, long-term convert and disciple of Christ.

OBSERVATIONS

One man, Erastus, is a traveling companion of Paul who is known for helping him. That alone is a significant designation and yet he is mentioned ten years later, exhibiting that their relationship has been longstanding and of some consequence. On the other hand, the person of Aristarchus appears to have become a believer through Paul's ministry and not only travels with him, but suffers with him. He endures gospel rejection with him and also joins him, by association at the least, as a partner in prison with him. He too may have been a "faithful friend" of Paul's for almost ten years. Gospel friendship and disciple investing relationships often provide long-term support and bonds that unite the members of the body of Christ in such special ways that they bear mentioning. Often, those mentioned are referred to by name and always with fondness!

Questions for Discussion

1. Paul describes Erastus as one of his helpers. Why is the role or the gift of "helping" (1 Cor 12:28) so valuable in the ministry of the church?

2. What would be missing in the ministry of the church if the gift of helps did not exist? Should the phrase "church volunteer" be replaced by the phrase "church helper"? What are the perceived differences in those terms?

3. Who is the most helpful person/believer you know? How have you observed/experienced their ministry or gift of helping?

4. Aristarchus is seized during a riot and also goes to prison with Paul. In what ways might we suffer persecution for our faith today? In what ways can we be co-sufferers with others? Can you provide an example of one believer suffering through the trials of another believer?

12

Priscilla and Aquila

Dynamic Duo

IN ACTS 18, LUKE tells us,

> "After this Paul left Athens and went to Corinth. ² And he found a Jew named Aquila, a native of Pontus, recently come from Italy with his wife Priscilla, because Claudius had commanded all the Jews to leave Rome. And he went to see them, ³ and because he was of the same trade he stayed with them and worked, for they were tentmakers by trade. ⁴ And he reasoned in the synagogue every Sabbath, and tried to persuade Jews and Greeks." (Acts 18:1–4)

Thus begins (AD 50) Paul's relationship with a dynamic duo, possibly the church's first power couple. And the woman has as high a profile as the man, if not higher!

This couple watches Paul reason with both Jews and Greeks at the synagogue week after week and they spend a considerable amount of time with the apostle since he remains in Corinth for some time (Acts 18:18). Eventually (eighteen months later), they travel with Paul to Ephesus. When they arrive, they settle into the city along with Paul. As tentmakers, they are able to maintain their living (well enough to have a home of some sort in the city) and remain with/under Paul's ministry. They continue to watch as Paul reasons once again with the Jews in the synagogue on a regular basis. Paul is asked to remain in the area but he declines and is determined to move on, possibly confident that he has left this ministry in the good hands of Priscilla and Aquila (Acts 18:19).

Sometime later, this gifted couple hears Apollos and are quite impressed with his bold synagogue speaking. Realizing that his message is truncated in its gospel import, they invite him to their home and explain the way of God more adequately to him, filling in some missing gaps of Christ-centered preaching (Acts 18:26). It certainly appears that both Priscilla and Aquila are capable of instructing Apollos in the finer points of what is often called historical-redemptive thinking (simply stated, finding Christ in the Old Testament).

While in Ephesus (AD 54–55), Paul writes his first letter to the Corinthians and states, "The churches of Asia send you greetings. Aquila and Priscilla, together with the church in their house, send you hearty greetings in the Lord" (1 Cor 16:19). So we see that the church in Ephesus is meeting in their home and Priscilla and Aquila are among those who deliberately issue fond greetings to the Corinthian believers whom they know quite well.

When writing to the church at Rome two years later (AD 56–57), Paul says, "Greet Priscilla and Aquila, my fellow workers in Christ Jesus, 4 who risked their necks for my life, to whom not only I give thanks but all the churches of the Gentiles give thanks as well" (Rom 16:3–4). What they have done to risk their lives on Paul's behalf is not known. However, it appears that the act is common knowledge among the Gentile churches, as believing onlookers understand and are grateful for their efforts on behalf of the Apostle. Finally, as Paul faces the end of his life and writes the conclusion of his last letter ever (AD 64), he asks Timothy to greet Priscilla and Aquila (2 Tim 4:19). This vibrant, Christ-honoring couple cannot easily be forgotten.

Observations

In Priscilla and Aquila, we view a wife and husband team who have most certainly been discipled and taught by the Apostle Paul and who, in turn, disciple invest in the gifted but knowledge lacking orator Apollos. Here is a couple that loves Paul, as well as the young believers in Corinth to the extent that they clearly express it. Their home is available for the church! And when it comes to Paul, their love for him is deep enough to risk their lives on his behalf. What a beautiful picture of mutual love among those involved in the disciple investing process. Using the ministry of hospitality, both the sharing of their lives and their knowledge builds the kingdom of Christ in the initial stages of its infancy.

Questions for Discussion

1. Priscilla and Aquila invite Apollos to their home in order to help him understand the Scriptures. Recognizing that hospitality was practiced as a way of life in the first century, in what ways can we use our homes or our hospitality today to minister to other believers or people with spiritual and/or physical needs?

2. How does home hospitality differ from a breakfast or lunch out at a restaurant?

3. What do you think it would be like to have a church meeting in your home?

4. Priscilla and Aquila observe Paul's ministry of reasoning through the Scriptures with both the Jews and Greeks. What do you think "reasoning" with others means and how do we do it?

5. Can you think of some Scriptures in the Old Testament that speak of Christ? What are those passages and what do they say about his first coming?

6. Who has participated with your Christian life and walk in such a way that they are not easily forgotten?

13

Apollos

Well-Groomed Proclaimer

APOLLOS IS A DISCIPLE who surfaces suddenly in the narrative of the book of Acts. In chapter 18, Luke writes of him,

> "Now a Jew named Apollos, a native of Alexandria, came to Ephesus. He was an eloquent man, competent in the Scriptures. [25] He had been instructed in the way of the Lord. And being fervent in spirit, he spoke and taught accurately the things concerning Jesus, though he knew only the baptism of John. [26] He began to speak boldly in the synagogue, but when Priscilla and Aquila heard him, they took him aside and explained to him the way of God more accurately." (Acts 18:24–26)

Apparently Paul had been in Ephesus with Priscilla and Aquila whom he had met earlier in Corinth (Acts 18:1–4). But he leaves them behind in Ephesus and is gone just prior to Apollos's arrival (Acts 18:18–22). Whether directly or indirectly, Paul disciple invests in Priscilla and Aquila who in turn invest in Apollos, this occurring in their own home.

Paul leaves Ephesus and sails on to Caesarea, Jerusalem, and eventually Antioch. From Antioch, he travels to Galatia and Phrygia in order to follow-up with the believers in those locations. "In the meantime" (as Luke proposes), Apollos shows up in Ephesus where he encounters Priscilla and Aquila and they invest themselves in him. Then Luke writes,

> [27] And when he [Apollos] wished to cross to Achaia, the brothers encouraged him and wrote to the disciples to welcome him. When he arrived, he greatly helped those who through grace had

> believed, [28] for he powerfully refuted the Jews in public, showing by the Scriptures that the Christ was Jesus. (Acts 18:27–28)

Apollos is especially effective, now that he understands the gospel and how Jesus fulfills the Old Testament Scriptures. He is quite the traveling evangelist and apologist. However, while Apollos is in Corinth, Paul has returned to Ephesus (Acts 19:1). They continue to miss each other in their respective travels. Paul's original visit to Corinth occurs in AD 51 (Acts 18:1–17) and then Apollos visits Corinth on the trip mentioned in Acts 19:1 (AD 53–54).

Indeed, Paul writes to the Corinthians about their many congregational divisions and disunity in AD 54, saying, "What I mean is that each one of you says, 'I follow Paul,' or 'I follow Apollos,' or 'I follow Cephas,' or 'I follow Christ'" (1 Cor 1:12). He follows up this concept, saying,

> But I, brothers, could not address you as spiritual people, but as people of the flesh, as infants in Christ. [2] I fed you with milk, not solid food, for you were not ready for it. And even now you are not yet ready, [3] for you are still of the flesh. For while there is jealousy and strife among you, are you not of the flesh and behaving only in a human way? [4] For when one says, "I follow Paul," and another, "I follow Apollos," are you not being merely human? [5] What then is Apollos? What is Paul? Servants through whom you believed, as the Lord assigned to each. [6] I planted, Apollos watered, but God gave the growth. [7] So neither he who plants nor he who waters is anything, but only God who gives the growth. [8] He who plants and he who waters are one, and each will receive his wages according to his labor. [9] For we are God's fellow workers. You are God's field, God's building. (1 Cor 3:1–9)

Apollos has certainly had a spiritual impact on these believers. He has taught them so effectively (and probably more impressively than even the Apostle Paul), that some of them have sided with his teaching and/or personality. Yet, Paul reminds the Corinthian believers that each laborer among them is only an instrument in God's hands. Paul also writes of Apollos (among other passages), "I have applied all these things to myself and Apollos for your benefit, brothers, that you may learn by us not to go beyond what is written, that none of you may be puffed up in favor of one against another" (1 Cor 4:6).

The Corinthians were led to the Lord by Paul. Paul stayed in Corinth for quite some time (Acts 18:18), so we know that he has been a disciple investor in their lives. Paul disciples and invests in Priscilla and Aquila.

They subsequently invest in Apollos's understanding of both Jesus and the Scriptures. Apollos later invests in the Corinthians when he visits them. The Corinthians do not fully understand that ultimately they are *God's* cultivated field (1 Cor 3:9) or that ultimately each of them is being discipled by Jesus himself, through his chosen instruments, in his chosen time.

Finally, although we are not completely certain when Paul and Apollos crossed paths and became friends and co-laborers in the gospel enterprise, we know at some point they built an association that went beyond their mutual association with Priscilla and Aquila. Paul writes at the end of his first letter to the Corinthian church, "Now concerning our brother Apollos, I strongly urged him to visit you with the other brothers, but it was not at all his will to come now. He will come when he has opportunity" (1 Cor 16:12). Paul indicates that he has had personal contact and conversation with Apollos and also calls him his brother. However, Apollos's desire not to visit Corinth appears to be unusual. The theory for his reticence toward the visit is that, because of his powerful speaking abilities and the division his presence has cast upon the church, he doesn't want to return. Paul must coax him to go back, another example of disciple investing.

Lastly, Paul writes Titus and charges him, "Do your best to speed Zenas the lawyer and Apollos on their way; see that they lack nothing" (Titus 3:13). Paul has sent Apollos on another journey, surely a gospel journey. We don't know where he is going but he will pass through Crete, so Paul pushes Titus to do all he can to assist him on his way. In Apollos, we see another minister and co-worker in the gospel willing to travel at the bidding of the apostle. In doing so, Paul will be sure to help this valuable disciple along the way. One is left to wonder, "Did Apollos, benefiting from the influence of Paul, write the book of Hebrews?"

Observations

In the life and ministry of Apollos, we have the picture of a chain of disciple investing: Paul invests in a married couple of disciples, Priscilla and Aquila, and they in turn invest in Apollos, an obviously gifted speaker and communicator. Apollos has the motivation, the fervor, the exceptional blessing of being able to speak publicly, and enough knowledge of Jesus to at least proclaim his name. We might wonder if in some way, he has been discipled by John the Baptist's preaching and simply needed more discipling along the way. Possibly, in Apollos, we have a picture of one planting

(John the Baptist) and others watering (Priscilla and Aquila), a beautiful portrait demonstrating the various methods Christ uses to disciple his followers. One (John the Baptist) invests through preaching, and then Christ brings others along to further personally invest in them, both investors conveying the necessary knowledge to help the disciple grow in Christ and to minister on behalf of Christ. Through the investment of Priscilla and Aquila, Apollos is equipped to be a more effective communicator of Christ than he already is. He has therefore now become more capable in order to properly invest in others, those who hear his message. He progresses so much that the church at Corinth not only benefits from his preaching but apparently they extol his leadership inappropriately. Paul has to remind them that Apollos, as effective as he is, remains only a servant of Christ and ultimately, they are "God's cultivated field."

Questions for Discussion

1. Apollos is the fruit of Paul's disciple investing in Priscilla and Aquila. Can you think of anyone who has invested in your walk and also name someone who invested in their walk? If you know, how did your disciple investor benefit from the person who invested in them?

2. Paul has a high profile with the church at Corinth and Apollos apparently is held in similar regard by the Corinthian Christians. How do we, as Christians, avoid dividing one another over different Christian leaders, speakers, and pastors?

3. How does Paul's relationship with Apollos demonstrate Paul's own humility as a leader?

4. Capitalizing on the famous first words of an evangelism method known as "The Four Spiritual Laws," someone once aptly stated, "Christian manipulation occurs when your leader tells you, 'God loves you and *I* have a wonderful plan for your life!'" Interestingly, Paul tells us that he cajoled or strongly urged Apollos to visit the Corinthian church, but it was not his will to go. How do believers tend to manipulate others to do *their* will and how do we learn to *allow* others to seek the Lord's will for their lives? What is Christian freedom, how is it defined biblically, and how do we practice it in the body of Christ?

14

Luke

Physician, Faithful to the End

LUKE, OF COURSE, IS the author of both the gospel named after him and the written account of the continuing history of the church that Jesus founded known as the book of Acts. Luke is usually assumed to originate from Antioch and is an early Gentile convert of the first Gentile church. He is a doctor, as noted in Colossians 4:14, "Luke the beloved physician greets you, as does Demas." He is apparently Paul's physician and traveling companion and first appears in the books of Acts at Troas (Acts 16). Note the change of third person to first person in this passage:

> [6] And *they* [Paul and his companions] went through the region of Phrygia and Galatia, having been forbidden by the Holy Spirit to speak the word in Asia. [7] And when they had come up to Mysia, they attempted to go into Bithynia, but the Spirit of Jesus did not allow them. [8] So, passing by Mysia, they went down to Troas. [9] And a vision appeared to Paul in the night: a man of Macedonia was standing there, urging him and saying, "Come over to Macedonia and help us." [10] And when Paul had seen the vision, immediately *we* sought to go on into Macedonia, concluding that God had called us to preach the gospel to them. (Acts 16:6–10, italics mine for emphasis)

Without doing a thorough study of the book of Acts, Luke's presence can be noted by this shifting from a third-person narrative to a first-person narrative throughout the remainder of the book. Evidently, Luke records many firsthand experiences and spends an elaborate amount of time with the apostle Paul, whom F.F. Bruce says is "Luke's hero!"[1]

As a physician, Luke is well-educated. He is also considered to be the earliest of the Christian apologists. In verse 10 above, it appears that Luke considers himself an evangelist, along with Paul. He writes both the gospel named after him and the book of Acts as an accurate researcher and historian. An ever faithful companion and truly a believer in Christ, Luke is with Paul in both of his imprisonments. He is with Paul while he is under Roman house arrest, as seen in Philemon 1:23–24, "Epaphras, my fellow prisoner in Christ Jesus, sends greetings to you, [24] and so do Mark, Aristarchus, Demas, and Luke, my fellow workers." And Paul mentions him, in his final writings, as his only remaining companion while he suffers under Roman imprisonment in a dark, damp dungeon in an unknown location, "Luke alone is with me. Get Mark and bring him with you, for he is very useful to me for ministry" (2 Tim 4:11).

Observations

Luke was undoubtedly a disciple of Paul's although we might determine that the disciple investing relationship was rather organic. Luke "hangs around" Paul during his travels, cares for him in his physical struggles and imprisonments, learns from him, and preaches the gospel with him. And if we wonder about the impact Paul has upon Luke, we need only look at the "time kept" historical books known as The Gospel of Luke and the Acts of the Apostles. As Luke has been captured by the gospel, so he has captured the stories of both Christ and his church. His writings have produced Christ followers for centuries!

Questions for Discussion

1. What do you think it would be like to have your doctor as your traveling companion?
2. What kind of relationship do you think would develop between a person suffering from a medical condition and a person who is giving them constant medical attention and help?

1. Bruce, *Acts*, 29.

3. What do you think "organic" (i. e., occurring naturally) disciple investing (as opposed to a program one follows) would look like in today's world?

4. If you invest in another person's growth in Christian faith and service, how do you evaluate whether or not they are replicating the life and ministry of Christ in others as well (as Luke does with his writing)?

15

Mark

Restored and Useful

Simply stated, Mark's relationship with Paul is not an explicitly positive one, and references to it are brief. In Acts 12:12, Mark (also called John) appears at the house of his mother, Mary, which is Peter's destination upon his miraculous escape from prison. Later in that chapter, he is mentioned as a traveling companion of Barnabas and Saul/Paul (Acts 12:25) and shows up on the first missionary journey as a traveling "helper" (Acts 13:5). According to Colossians 4:10, Mark is Barnabas's cousin. Barnabas talks Paul into taking Mark with them on the first missionary journey, but Mark turns back seemingly to retreat to Jerusalem (Acts 13:13). Luke does not explain this sudden departure to the reader.

After the Jerusalem Council, however, Luke tells us,

> [36] And after some days Paul said to Barnabas, "Let us return and visit the brothers in every city where we proclaimed the word of the Lord, and see how they are." [37] Now Barnabas wanted to take with them John called Mark. [38] But Paul thought best not to take with them one who had withdrawn from them in Pamphylia and had not gone with them to the work. [39] And there arose a sharp disagreement, so that they separated from each other. Barnabas took Mark with him and sailed away to Cyprus, [40] but Paul chose Silas and departed, having been commended by the brothers to the grace of the Lord. [41] And he went through Syria and Cilicia, strengthening the churches. (Acts 15:36–41)

The crucial and demanding nature of the missionary journeys makes Paul's willingness to bring along an apparent deserter untenable in his own mind. The two missionary teammates split up as Barnabas takes his cousin, John Mark, with him (AD 49). We do not hear anything else about Mark throughout the book of Acts, as Paul's journeys, without question, take precedence over any efforts or travels of Barnabas and John Mark. However, in time, the dispute with Barnabas is placed in the past, as Paul refers to Mark in three different letters. At the end of his epistle to the Colossians Paul writes, "Aristarchus my fellow prisoner greets you, and Mark the cousin of Barnabas (concerning whom you have received instructions—if he comes to you, welcome him)" (Col 4:10). Here we realize that some twelve years later (AD 60–61), Paul supports Mark's involvement in ministry.

And in the companion letter to the Colossians, i.e., the letter to Philemon, Paul writes that Mark is a fellow worker, a great word of commendation from one in whom the apostle had little trust many years earlier. Then, a few years later, Paul writes from prison, near the end of his life (AD 64) in his second letter to Timothy, "Luke alone is with me. Get Mark and bring him with you, for he is very useful to me for ministry" (2 Tim 4:11). At the end of his life, Paul obviously wants Mark by his side because he believes in him. He has become convinced that Mark will ultimately live up to his initial potential in the days from that original missionary journey. For many years, Mark may not have been Paul's disciple. However, at the end of his life, the aging apostle has recognized that another man's (or men's) disciple investing in this youngster has paid off and ultimately, Paul can become the benefactor!

Observations

Many scholars believe that Mark is the young man in the Garden of Gethsemane who was wearing nothing but a linen garment and following Jesus at his arrest (Mark 14:51–52). When Jesus was seized, he (Mark) fled naked, leaving his garment behind. We do not know the answer to this assertion but if he is a fearful type, we would notice a pattern in the life of a young man, as one who is tempted to run from pressurized situations. Mark is, however, assumed to be the writer (or mouthpiece) of Peter's version of the gospel, as their relationship is stated in 1 Peter 5:13, where Peter writes, "She who is at Babylon, who is likewise chosen, sends you greetings, and so does Mark, my son." Peter has obviously taken Mark in as a son of the faith and possibly Peter has become his mentor or discipler due to his proximity to his family (see Acts 12:12). Despite Paul's initial concerns for Mark's weak constitution, both Barnabas and Peter value him. In my opinion, with Mark, we learn the ever faithful lessons, "The Lord takes care of his own" and "Jesus is the ultimate discipler of his people."

Questions for Discussion

1. How do you handle personal failure? What are the biblical solutions for failure?

2. How do you handle rejection? How would you feel if a very important person argued that you were not useful for their purposes? Where do you turn when you are rejected?

3. How would you handle being the center of a personal dispute or conflict between two other people? What would you do if you were on the losing side?

4. How does Paul demonstrate that he holds no grudges against Mark for his past failure and apparent withdrawal from an earlier mission trip?

5. What do we know about Jesus that encourages us to move forward after a personal failure that disappoints others?

Conclusion

As we consider the concept of disciple investing and the number of disciples, associates, and partners with whom the Apostle Paul is affiliated, the overwhelming conclusion is that Paul invested in more people than we can imagine. Paul has influenced both men and women for the sake of Christ and his kingdom. Paul obviously took Timothy aside as a very young man and a recent convert to Christ and focused a considerable amount of attention upon him. Yet, Paul spends quality time with groups of people as well as with various disciples whom he considers teammates or co-workers. He disciples seasoned leaders and new converts. He relies upon the help and personal presence of others. He preaches, teaches, evangelizes, encourages, charges, and pastors others.

Additionally, he writes authoritatively, yet often with love, compassion, and tenderness while building people up in the faith and resolving conflict and other problems. He is investing in others at all times, seemingly all the time. Even when he makes tents, he has Priscilla and Aquila at his side. Disciple investing, in the life of Paul, is simply letting Christ live in and through a believer and then making him the focus of all that person does, while helping others to move toward him and pointing others to him so that they might become like him and know him more fully. The bottom line is that disciple investing, or the approach of seeking to introduce *everyone* to a life filled with Christ, is a way of life for the Apostle Paul. As those who are called to follow Christ, every believer, whether serving in full time ministry or not, should seek to invest in the lives of others, so that they may know Christ, become like Christ, and live their lives for the glory and honor of Christ. May the great discipler of his people give us the grace to do so! Amen!

Appendix One

Paul and His Investment in "Many Others"

THERE ARE A NUMBER of other associates who appear in the book of Acts and in the Pauline epistles. These individuals are more or less significant in Paul's life, and whether great or small, each plays a part in his life and ministry. I have listed them in *alphabetical* order and have made observational comments when beneficial:

1. Ampliatus, Paul's dear friend in the Lord (Rom 16:8).

2. Andronicus and Junia, Paul's fellow Jews who have been in prison with him; they are outstanding among the apostles, and were in Christ before he was (Rom 16:7). It is significant to note that these two believers had a good reputation among the first century apostles, and were long time believers whose maturity was demonstrated by the fact that they suffered imprisonment with Paul for the sake of the gospel and possibly for the sake of their association with him.

3. Apelles, whose fidelity to Christ has stood the test (Rom 16:10), what a blessed description of any believer: tested, but faithful to Christ through the trial. All disciples of Jesus should be so described!

4. Apphia, Philemon's wife (Phlm 2).

5. Archippus, a fellow worker/soldier (Phlm 2); Paul tells him in Colossians 4:17, "See that you fulfill the ministry that you have received in the Lord." This kingdom laborer fights for the expansion of Christ's spiritual kingdom and lest he become weary, he is admonished to continue in the ministry given him by the Lord!

6. Aristobulus and those belonging to his household (Rom 16:10).

7. Artemas and Tychicus, those whom Paul would send to aid Titus in his pastoral duties, allowing him to attend to/visit Paul (Titus 3:12).

8. Asyncritus, Phlegon, Hermes, Patrobas, Hermas and the other brothers and sisters with them (Rom 16:14).

9. Clement, who contended for the cause of the gospel, alongside Paul; as the gospel spawns conflict, Clement stands with Paul in the midst of the battle. Clement is joined by other co-laborers: unnamed gospel warriors who together have assurance that because they stand with the Apostle Paul in his defense of the gospel, their names are written in the book of life. Regardless of cost or circumstances, their eternal life is sealed (Phil 4:2–3).

10. Demas (and Paul's dear friend, Luke) who send greetings (Col 4:14; Phlm 24).

11. Epaenetus, Paul's dear friend, significantly marked as the first convert to Christ in the Asian province (Rom 16:5); what a blessing to be able to name an individual who came to Christ during an early (and I'm sure hopeful) missionary journey. Epaenetus's name should be known throughout the ages, and he certainly appears to have endeared himself to the Apostle who led him to the Christ of his salvation.

12. Erastus, the city's director of public works, and brother in the faith, Quartus, send Rome their greetings (Rom 16:23).

13. Eubulus greets Timothy, as do Pudens, Linus, Claudia, and all the brothers and sisters (2 Tim 4:21).

14. Euodia and Syntyche, women in the Philippian church with whom Paul pleads, desiring them to be of the same mind in the Lord; Paul asks his true companion[1] to help these women because of their contention in the cause of the gospel, along with Clement and other co-laborers, whose names are in the book of life (Phil 4:2–3). Paul knows them by name and loves them enough to publicly rebuke them for their conflict, especially because they have worked with him as he labors for the gospel.

15. Gaius, whose hospitality is enjoyed by Paul and the whole of the church in Rome, sends his greetings (Rom 16:23). Hospitality is a memorable

---

1. ... or *Syzgus*, from the Greek meaning "true yokefellow."

APPENDIX ONE

gift and Paul cannot help but mention this vital ministry of Gaius. Would that we might be more hospitable in gospel ministry.

16. Gaius from Derbe, Paul's companion on his third missionary journey; Macedonians Gaius and Aristarchus, are seized along with Paul during the riot in Ephesus (Acts 19:29; 20:4). Gaius is marked as a significant friend of Paul simply because he was seized when the riot in Ephesus broke out. Present with Paul but pulled away by the crowd, Paul's heart is to enter the crowd to retrieve Gaius; and although Paul is restrained in the midst of the chaos, his passion to regain his gospel companion demonstrates the depth of their relationship.

17. Herodion, a fellow Jew with Paul (Rom 16:11).

18. Jesus, who is called Justus, also sends greetings. These (Aristarcus, Mark, and Justus) are the only Jews among Paul's co-workers for the kingdom of God, and they have proved to be a comfort to him (Col 4:11).

19. Mary, who worked very hard for the Roman church (Rom 16:6); gospel ministry is never easy and Paul mentions a woman in Rome who apparently has demonstrated the ability to work hard for the benefit of her local church in Rome. Knowing how hard the Apostle Paul works, we can assume that this is no light compliment regarding her efforts for Christ.

20. Narcissus and those in that household of who are in the Lord (Rom 16:11).

21. Persis, Paul's beloved friend, another woman who has worked very hard in the Lord (Rom 16:12); it is interesting to note that just as Paul characterizes Mary as one who works hard for the Lord, just a few verses earlier, so he does for Persis. Yet he calls Persis "beloved," indicating that she is either well loved by the Apostle or by the church at Rome or both. Apparently, her hard work for the sake of the gospel is complemented by a personality that generates affection among those who know her.

22. Philologus, Julia, Nereus and his sister, and Olympas, and all the Lord's people who are with them (Rom 16:15).

23. Phoebe, a sister and deacon (or servant) of the church in Cenchreae, commended by Paul; Paul asks the Roman church to receive her in the Lord in a way worthy of his people and to give her any help she may need from them, for she has been the benefactor of many people,

including Paul (Rom 16:1–2). Phoebe is a woman with a servant's heart. Some believe she was a deaconess (female deacon), and although that conclusion is debatable, she was most definitely a woman who served the Lord, as she has not only assisted Paul (monetarily it appears), but others as well. Paul honors Phoebe by naming her first in his list of Roman associates, affectionately calling her "sister," and commending both her service and generosity.

24. Rufus, chosen in the Lord, and his mother, who has been a mother to Paul as well (Rom 16:13); Paul is apparently convinced that Rufus is God's man, chosen by him for whatever reasons. Rufus's mother, unnamed, must be a special woman because, in somewhat unusual fashion for Paul, he states that she has cared for him like a mother, extending her affection and interest from Rufus to the Apostle. This description of Rufus's mother is another indication of the warm side of Paul's heart.

25. Sopater, son of Pyrrhus from Berea, a companion of Paul on his third missionary journey (Acts 20:4).

26. Secundus from Thessalonica, a companion of Paul on his third missionary journey (Acts 20:4).

27. Stephanas and his household of whom were the first converts in Achaia; they have devoted themselves to the service of the Lord's people. Paul urges the Corinthian brothers and sisters to submit to such people and to everyone who joins in their work and labors. Stephanas is also an individual who visits Paul while he ministers in Ephesus, and in doing so, refreshes the Apostle's spirit (1 Cor 16:15–16). Do you think Paul noticed when someone came to true faith in Christ? What about an entire household (probably a family with children and maybe servants and extended family)? What about the first converts in an entire region? Paul's ministry was validated by such early conversion responses! How does he know that they are converts? The answer is plain—devotion to God's service and his people, and a willingness to visit with the Apostle, thus encouraging him in spirit!

28. Tertius, who wrote down this letter (Rom), greets the church at Rome in the Lord (Rom 16:22).

29. Stephanas (above), Fortunatus, and Achaicus, men who made Paul glad when they arrived because they supplied what was lacking from

APPENDIX ONE

the Corinthians; they refreshed Paul's spirit and that of the Corinthian church. Such men deserve recognition (1 Cor 16:17–18). Here are three men who took the time to travel from Corinth to Ephesus (a journey of 354 miles by land and eight days by sea), thus demonstrating their response to the gospel and interest in the preacher of the gospel, their beloved Apostle Paul. Their arrival and presence made him glad and refreshed his spirit. Theirs was truly a ministry of mutual disciple investing.

30. Tryphena and Tryphosa, women who worked hard in the Lord (Rom 16:12); the Apostle Paul obviously extols women who work hard for the Lord. These two women's efforts on behalf of the gospel have not gone unnoticed. Apparently, Paul has personally observed their efforts for the Lord or has at least heard about the fruit of their labors.

31. Urbanus, a co-worker in Christ, and Paul's dear friend Stachys (Rom 16:9).

Observations

When we read a list such as this one and see the wide variety of people with whom the Apostle Paul associated, we recognize that the Paul is a man who has created quite a network of contacts. We view a man with many friends in a plethora of locations. Captured by the grace of Christ, Paul is a man on fire for building relationships that will move people toward the Savior. He has invested in the following: new converts to Christ, travelling companions, those he considers to be fellow laborers and soldiers in the spiritual battle, and even some whom he meets or suffers with while in prison. The list above also includes a variety of woman, many who work diligently for the gospel, one who exhibits servanthood in high capacity, some who need to get along better, as well as one friend's mother who functions in some ways as a mother to Paul himself. As an aggressor in gospel proclamation, the Apostle Paul meets and befriends scores of people and retains their names through the course of his manifold travels. While the nature of Paul's disciple investing is not always evident from these various passages, the extent is obvious. Paul has met, evangelized, and discipled people everywhere he has travelled.

Appendix Two

A Closer Look at Timothy and Titus

WHEN WE READ THE three letters Paul writes to two young pastors whom he has left in charge of their respective churches (Timothy in Ephesus and Titus in Crete), letters known as "the pastor epistles," we will discover that Paul appears to know these men and their situations very well. Much can be learned by studying the content of these (and other) letters with regard to Paul's relationship with both men and his expectations of these challenged pastors. The purpose of this appendix is to take a closer look at the interactions between Paul, Timothy, and Titus.

Timothy in the Pauline Epistles

Paul mentions Timothy in a number of his letters, and the phrases Paul uses to describe this disciple shed further light on Timothy's character:

- **Romans 16:21**—"Timothy, my fellow worker, greets you; so do Lucius and Jason and Sosipater, my kinsmen."

In this passage, as Paul concludes his letter from Corinth to the Romans, he mentions that Timothy sends his greetings to the church at Rome, along with a few others who are more explicitly Jewish. The *Pulpit Commentary* states, "Timothy may have joined St. Paul at Corinth before the letter was finally sent, not having been with him when it was begun. For his name is not conjoined with St. Paul's in the opening salutation, as it is in 2 Corinthians

1:1; Philippians 1:1; Colossians 1:1; 1 Thessalonians 1:1; 2 Thessalonians 1:1."[1]

Significant, however, is the fact that Paul calls Timothy his *coworker*, a term designating that Timothy is a man of energy when it comes to supporting and working with Paul in gospel ministry and service.

- **1 Corinthians 4:17**—"That is why I sent you Timothy, my beloved and faithful child in the Lord, to remind you of my ways in Christ, as I teach them everywhere in every church."

In this brief communication, Paul writes a ringing endorsement of Timothy, whom he confidently believes will be a great benefit to the believers in Corinth. Timothy has become like *a son* to Paul, *deeply loved* and *dependable* or *faithful* in his allegiance to the Lord. Because of these attributes, Paul rests assured that when Timothy arrives, he will not only capably support Paul's credibility in Christian service but will be able to underscore the consistent teaching of Paul throughout the churches touched by his ministry. The bonding of the hearts and minds of these two men, as suggested by this passage, is a powerful testimony of disciple-investing process and the fruit it bears.

- **1 Corinthians 16:10ff**—"When Timothy comes, see that you put him at ease among you, for he is doing the work of the Lord, as I am. [11] So let no one despise him. Help him on his way in peace, that he may return to me, for I am expecting him with the brothers."

Paul closes his first letter to the Corinthians with another reference to the coming of Timothy. The letter has been difficult to write, has included numerous rebukes and admonitions, and apparently Paul is concerned about how "his representative" will be received by these "spanked" believers. In addition, Timothy, as well trained as he has been by the apostle and as active as he has been in his in co-laboring with Paul, has demonstrated a weaker (and possibly more fearful) constitution. Thus his trip to Corinth is one of possible anxiety due to a nature that is sensitive to intimidation. Paul believes in and trusts Timothy to carry his mantle to the Corinthian believers, but he is still concerned that when Timothy arrives, the smoldering fumes of pastoral rebuke might hinder the receptivity of his ministry there. Paul reminds them that Timothy is God's servant *carrying on the work of*

---

1. Spence, *II Corinthians*, 451.

the Lord as is Paul, although his ministry style (by implication) is different. Here is disciple delegation and disciple defense at its best!

- **2 Corinthians 1:1, 18–19**—"Paul, an apostle of Christ Jesus by the will of God, and Timothy our brother, to the church of God that is at Corinth, with all the saints who are in the whole of Achaia . . . [18] As surely as God is faithful, our word to you has not been Yes and No. [19] For the Son of God, Jesus Christ, whom we proclaimed among you, Silvanus and Timothy and I, was not Yes and No, but in him it is always Yes."

In these two texts, Timothy is included in the salutation and mentioned as our brother, noting that he is not only Paul's brother in Christ but a brother to the believers in Corinth. In verse 19, Paul writes that Timothy has been a preacher among the Corinthians like both Paul and Silas, preaching the Son of God, Jesus Christ. Surely, Paul must be proud to mention that Timothy has been faithful in preaching the gospel message as he himself has preached it.

- **Philippians 2:19–24**—"I hope in the Lord Jesus to send Timothy to you soon, so that I too may be cheered by news of you. [20] For I have no one like him, who will be genuinely concerned for your welfare. [21] For they all seek their own interests, not those of Jesus Christ. [22] But you know Timothy's proven worth, how as a son with a father he has served with me in the gospel. [23] I hope therefore to send him just as soon as I see how it will go with me, [24] and I trust in the Lord that shortly I myself will come also."

This is one of the most stirring passages on the personal level written by the Apostle Paul with regard to one of his co-laborers, and it merits significant remarks. It compares only to the next section of the letter to the church in Philippi in which Paul mentions the risk-taking behavior of Epaphroditus. Paul has so often sent Timothy on journeys or left him behind to take care of various church affairs that the reader readily recognizes he has become Paul's right-hand man.

The Apostle knows that this beloved congregation is awaiting the news of the verdict regarding his imprisonment (most probably in Rome). But he wishes them to know that his regard for their well-being is mutual. Epaphroditus, a member of the Philippian church, has come as a liaison of or representative from the church, carrying with him a generous gift from these faithful believers. Hendriksen surmises that Epaphroditus's journey would normally take at least one month but due to his illness and other encumbrances, the trip most likely took at least two.[2] Apparently, Paul is responding to the return of Epaphroditus from Philippi, but has received news that this first messenger has gotten ill, sick almost unto the point of death. The Jamieson-Fausset-Brown Bible Commentary states,

> From Php 2:19-30, it appears Epaphroditus was to set out at once to allay the anxiety of the Philippians on his [Paul's] account, and at the same time bearing the Epistle; Timothy was to follow after the apostle's liberation was decided, when they could arrange their plans more definitely as to where Timothy should, on his return with tidings from Philippi, meet Paul, who was designing by a wider circuit, and slower progress, to reach that city. Paul's reason for sending Timothy so soon after having heard of the Philippians from Epaphroditus was that they were now suffering persecutions (Php 1:28-30); and besides, Epaphroditus' delay through sickness on his journey to Rome from Philippi, made the tidings he brought to be of less recent date than Paul desired. Paul himself also hoped to visit them shortly.[3]

Paul responds that in addition to sending Epaphroditus back to them (most probably the carrier of the epistle), in return he will soon send Timothy to encourage them in their spiritual progress as they face newfound persecution. In this passage, Paul demonstrates that he is fully reliant on the Lord's will for employing Timothy in the service of the church at Philippi. He also displays confidence that he can send Timothy and expect Timothy to return with a report of good news about the church. He knows that in sending Timothy, he has a kindred soul, one who is like-minded, a fellow worker who has a true pastor's heart—Timothy's concerns are both genuine and others-centered. Unlike others whom Paul has observed, Timothy seeks only those interests that belong to Jesus Christ. Timothy is not self-invested or even seeking primarily to fulfill Paul's interests. Timothy is about Jesus Christ! Paul's reflections upon Timothy's behavior are evident as he has observed Timothy time and time again. Paul has watched Timothy in gospel service much like a parent does his child; he knows Timothy's value because he has proven himself over time in the work of the gospel.

2. Hendriksen, *Philippians*, 17–8.
3. Jamieson, *Commentary*, 431.

- **1 Thessalonians 3:1-6**—"Therefore when we could bear it no longer, we were willing to be left behind at Athens alone, [2] and we sent Timothy, our brother and God's coworker in the gospel of Christ, to establish and exhort you in your faith, [3] that no one be moved by these afflictions. For you yourselves know that we are destined for this. [4] For when we were with you, we kept telling you beforehand that we were to suffer affliction, just as it has come to pass, and just as you know. [5] For this reason, when I could bear it no longer, I sent to learn about your faith, for fear that somehow the tempter had tempted you and our labor would be in vain. [6] But now that Timothy has come to us from you, and has brought us the good news of your faith and love and reported that you always remember us kindly and long to see us, as we long to see you—."

Athens is no easy endeavor for the Apostle Paul; it is a city filled with idolatry and godlessness. He faces the challenges of a purely Greek world exhibiting not only sensual idolatry but pluralistic unbelief. Yet his heart is burdened for the young church in Thessalonica, enough so that he must part with his favored companion. Although the timetable of Timothy's exact origin of departure is debatable, Hendriksen writes a satisfactory view of the most possible timeline, "A probable view is that Timothy had left Berea and had found Paul while the latter was still in Athens; that Paul, anxious about the affairs of the church in Thessalonica, sent him back to the congregation in order to establish and comfort it . . ."[4] Hendriksen also states that this is "a sacrifice of love" on the part of the Apostle as he also had to send Silas to Macedonia at the same time, truly leaving himself alone.[5]

Timothy's preciousness to a heart-wrenched Paul is evident in the expressions he uses to characterize the younger disciple. He is a *brother*, a *coworker in God's service*, one who *spreads the gospel of Christ*, and is *able to strengthen and encourage* them in their faith. Paul is confident that Timothy will be an asset to these believers' faith. And upon Timothy's return (verse 6), Paul is overjoyed as he hears that, despite the reality of opposition facing these believers personally in Thessalonica (3:1-5), he has received good news about both their faith and their love. He has been praying night and day (9-10) and his prayers have been answered!

---

4. Hendriksen, *Thessalonians*, 82-3
5. Ibid., 83.

APPENDIX TWO

Timothy in the Pauline Salutations

Below is a list of salutations that the Apostle Paul uses while either including Timothy or when writing to Timothy (in the Pastoral Epistles). I have noted any descriptors of Timothy if present in the salutation.

- **Philippians 1:1**—"Paul and Timothy, servants of Christ Jesus." In the salutation of the letter to the church at Philippi, Paul includes Timothy and calls him a *servant of Christ Jesus*, as he himself was.
- **Colossians 1:1**—"Paul, an apostle of Christ Jesus by the will of God, and Timothy *our brother*,"
- **1 Thessalonians 1:1**—"Paul, Silvanus and Timothy,"
- **2 Thessalonians 1:1**—"Paul, Silvanus and Timothy,"
- **1 Timothy 1:2**—"Paul, an apostle of Christ Jesus by command of God our Savior and of Christ Jesus our hope, ² To Timothy, *my true [genuine] child in the faith* . . ."
- **2 Timothy 1:2**—"Paul, an apostle of Christ Jesus by the will of God, according to the promise of life that is in Christ Jesus, To Timothy, *my beloved child* . . ."
- **Philemon 1**—"Paul, a prisoner for Christ Jesus, and Timothy *our brother* . . ."

Conclusion from the Pauline Epistles and Salutations

As we peruse the instances in which Paul mentions Timothy in his letters, as well as the salutations written by Paul in those letters, Paul's relationship to Timothy might be summarized as follows:

Timothy is a dear and true (or genuine) son in the faith, deeply loved by Paul and yet a brother of Paul and other believers, a coworker in God's service, like-minded with Paul, and faithful, a servant of Jesus Christ, carrying on the work of the Lord and proven with the work of the gospel, as one having a genuine concern for others' welfare, motivated with the interests of Jesus Christ in mind, a preacher of the Son of God, Jesus Christ, and one who spreads the gospel of Christ, able to strengthen and encourage others in their faith.

APPENDIX TWO

Observations

Here we see the fruit of disciple investing and particularly of "disciple companionship," i.e., serving Christ together. The relationship of Paul and Timothy has been forged in the midst of active, frontline ministry, including suffering and rejection. The relationship has become much like a father/son union, filled with deep love and devotion to one another. Paul recognizes that Timothy is first and foremost all about Jesus Christ and the gospel that proclaims him. He wants to see the good news of Jesus spread to others. Timothy has learned from Paul that the Christian life and pastoral ministry is about the welfare of others. The union of this vision for ministry has bonded them like brothers. Timothy has grown into a servant of Jesus who can now strengthen and encourage others in their faith and lead them as a pastor. This is disciple investing at its best!

Timothy and Pauline Admonitions (Pastoral Epistles)

The nature of a brief study such as this one forbids a full commentary on Paul's two Pastoral Epistles written to Timothy. However, I would like to take a few moments to survey these writings in order to scan the nature of the Paul/Timothy ministerial relationship and how Paul exhorts this young local church pastor (emphasis in italics):

- **1 Timothy 1:3–4**—"As I urged you when I was going to Macedonia, *remain at Ephesus* so that you may *charge certain persons not to teach any different doctrine,* [4] nor to devote themselves to myths and endless genealogies, which promote speculations rather than the stewardship from God that is by faith."

- **1 Timothy 1:18–20**—"This charge I entrust to you, Timothy, my child, in accordance with the prophecies previously made about you, that by them *you may wage the good warfare,* [19] *holding faith and a good conscience.* By rejecting this, some have made shipwreck of their faith, [20] among whom are Hymenaeus and Alexander, whom I have handed over to Satan that they may learn not to blaspheme."

- **1 Timothy 3:14–15**—"I hope to come to you soon, but I am writing these things to you so that, [15] if I delay, *you may know how one ought to behave in the household of God,* which is the church of the living God, a pillar and buttress of the truth."

- **1 Timothy 4:6–16**—"*If you put these things before the brothers*, you will be a good servant of Christ Jesus, being trained in the words of the faith and of the good doctrine that you have followed. ⁷ *Have nothing to do with irreverent, silly myths. Rather train yourself for godliness;* ⁸ for while bodily training is of some value, godliness is of value in every way, as it holds promise for the present life and also for the life to come. ⁹ The saying is trustworthy and deserving of full acceptance. ¹⁰ For to this end we toil and strive, because we have our hope set on the living God, who is the Savior of all people, especially of those who believe. ¹¹ *Command and teach these things.* ¹² Let no one despise you for your youth, *but set the believers an example in speech, in conduct, in love, in faith, in purity.* ¹³ Until I come, *devote yourself to the public reading of Scripture, to exhortation, to teaching.* ¹⁴ *Do not neglect the gift you have*, which was given you by prophecy when the council of elders laid their hands on you. ¹⁵ *Practice these things, immerse yourself in them*, so that all may see your progress. ¹⁶ *Keep a close watch on yourself and on the teaching. Persist in this*, for by so doing you will save both yourself and your hearers."

- **1 Timothy 6:2b–4a**—"*Teach and urge* these things. ³ If anyone teaches a different doctrine and does not agree with the sound words of our Lord Jesus Christ and the teaching that accords with godliness, ⁴ he is puffed up with conceit and understands nothing."

- **1 Timothy 6:11–15**—"¹¹ But as for you, O man of God, *flee these things. Pursue righteousness, godliness, faith, love, steadfastness, gentleness.* ¹² *Fight the good fight of the faith. Take hold of the eternal life* to which you were called and about which you made the good confession in the presence of many witnesses. ¹³ I charge you in the presence of God, who gives life to all things, and of Christ Jesus, who in his testimony before Pontius Pilate made the good confession, ¹⁴ *to keep the commandment unstained and free from reproach until the appearing of our Lord Jesus Christ,* ¹⁵ which he will display at the proper time—he who is the blessed and only Sovereign, the King of kings and Lord of lords, ¹⁶ who alone has immortality, who dwells in unapproachable light, whom no one has ever seen or can see. To him be honor and eternal dominion. Amen."

- **1 Timothy 6:20–21a**—"*O Timothy, guard the deposit entrusted to you. Avoid the irreverent babble and contradictions of what is falsely called 'knowledge,'* [21] for by professing it some have swerved from the faith."

- **2 Timothy 1:6–8**—"For this reason I remind you to *fan into flame the gift of God*, which is in you through the laying on of my hands, [7] for God gave us a spirit not of fear but of power and love and self-control. [8] Therefore do not be ashamed of the testimony about our Lord, nor of me his prisoner, but share in suffering for the gospel by the power of God."

- **2 Timothy 1:13–14**—"*Follow the pattern of the sound words* that you have heard from me, *in the faith and love that are in Christ Jesus*. [14] By the Holy Spirit who dwells within us, *guard the good deposit entrusted to you*."

- **2 Timothy 2:1–4**—"You then, my child, *be strengthened by the grace that is in Christ Jesus,* [2] *and what you have heard from me in the presence of many witnesses entrust to faithful men who will be able to teach others also.* [3] *Share in suffering* as a good soldier of Christ Jesus. [4] No soldier gets entangled in civilian pursuits, since his aim is to please the one who enlisted him."

- **2 Timothy 2:14–16**—"*Remind them of these things, and charge them before God not to quarrel about words,* which does no good, but only ruins the hearers. [15] Do your best to present yourself to God as one approved, a worker who has no need to be ashamed, rightly handling the word of truth. [16] *But avoid irreverent babble*, for it will lead people into more and more ungodliness."

- **2 Timothy 2:22–26**—"So flee youthful passions and pursue righteousness, faith, love, and peace, along with those who call on the Lord from a pure heart. [23] Have nothing to do with foolish, ignorant controversies; you know that they breed quarrels. [24] And the Lord's servant must not be quarrelsome but kind to everyone, able to teach, patiently enduring evil, [25] correcting his opponents with gentleness. God may perhaps grant them repentance leading to a knowledge of the truth, [26] and they may come to their senses and escape from the snare of the devil, after being captured by him to do his will."

- **2 Timothy 3:14–17**—"*But as for you, continue in what you have learned and have firmly believed,* knowing from whom you learned it

¹⁵ and how from childhood you have been acquainted with the sacred writings, which are able to make you wise for salvation through faith in Christ Jesus. ¹⁶ All Scripture is breathed out by God and profitable for teaching, for reproof, for correction, and for training in righteousness, ¹⁷ that the man of God may be complete, equipped for every good work."

- **2 Timothy 4:1-5**—"*I charge you in the presence of God and of Christ Jesus, who is to judge the living and the dead, and by his appearing and his kingdom: ² preach the word; be ready in season and out of season; reprove, rebuke, and exhort, with complete patience and teaching. ³ For the time is coming when people will not endure sound teaching, but having itching ears they will accumulate for themselves teachers to suit their own passions, ⁴ and will turn away from listening to the truth and wander off into myths. ⁵ As for you, always be sober-minded, endure suffering, do the work of an evangelist, fulfill your ministry.*"

- **2 Timothy 4:9-13, 21-22**—"*Do your best to come to me soon. ¹⁰ For Demas, in love with this present world, has deserted me and gone to Thessalonica. Crescens has gone to Galatia, Titus to Dalmatia. ¹¹ Luke alone is with me. Get Mark and bring him with you, for he is very useful to me for ministry. ¹² Tychicus I have sent to Ephesus. ¹³ When you come, bring the cloak that I left with Carpus at Troas, also the books, and above all the parchments . . . 21 Do your best to come before winter. Eubulus sends greetings to you, as do Pudens and Linus and Claudia and all the brothers. ²² The Lord be with your spirit. Grace be with you.*"

Conclusions from the Pauline Admonitions to Timothy

As we observe these personal letters, known as Pastoral Epistles, from the hand of the Apostle Paul to his protégé Timothy, we are able to draw some interesting conclusions. I will simply list some of the observations.

In the realm of *personal relationship*, Paul urges Timothy . . .

- In an apostolic (almost bishopric) fashion, to remain in Ephesus in order to pastor a very mature congregation (1.1:3). Timothy complies.
- To do his best to come to Paul quickly, for Demas, because he has loved this world, has deserted Paul and has gone to Thessalonica. Crescens has gone to Galatia, and Titus to Dalmatia. Only Luke is with

Paul; therefore, Timothy is to get Mark and bring him with Timothy, because he is helpful to Paul in his ministry. Paul has sent Tychicus to Ephesus. When he comes, Paul wants Timothy to bring the cloak that he left with Carpus at Troas, and Paul's scrolls, especially the parchments. He appeals to Timothy to do his best to get there before winter (2.4:9–13, 21).

Observations

From the first letter of Paul to Timothy, we see that the trust and confidence that Paul (the disciple investor) has in Timothy (the disciple) has grown significantly and is demonstrated incredibly by the local church pastorate to which he appoints him. Timothy, (although not exemplifying the strongest constitution—he is sometimes known as "Timid Timothy"—see 2 Tim 1:3–5) willingly remains in Ephesus at Paul's request. Hendriksen remarks, "His [Timothy's] character was a blend of *amiability* and *faithfulness in spite of natural* timidity. Paul loved Timothy and admired his outstanding personality traits."[6] In the second letter to Timothy, we observe that Paul is facing the end of his life, presently imprisoned in a dark, damp prison cell that amounts to a hole in the ground with an opening for light and access for food delivery. He appears to long for Timothy to be with him, whether for companionship or possibly closure in the waning moments of the relationship. With the exception of Luke, his friend and physician, Paul is very much alone. Timothy apparently has access to some of Paul's belongings and valuables, scrolls and parchments for reading (ever the student), and a cloak for comfort in the chilly cell.

How close is their personal bond of love? Paul strongly petitions Timothy to come during his time of impending death; he needs Timothy with him. He is about to hand off the baton of ministry responsibility to him. Even though Timothy has seen Paul persecuted, beaten, threatened, and imprisoned under house arrest, he now needs to be present for this apparent worst situation of the apostle's life. How close has this mentor/mentee relationship become? We might well ask this question: "Who will show up at your funeral?" We know well the answer: those individuals that mean the most in our lives. These lasting friendships are displayed by the people who feel the real grief of losing us. Surely this is the sort of friendship shared between Paul and Timothy. We cannot imagine the depth of mutual love that

---

6. Hendriksen, *Pastoral*, 34.

exists between these two men. What stories they could tell! What memories they shared together! What knitting of hearts they must have experienced! Paul writes, "Do your best . . ." These words are actually a weak translation in the ESV. The phrase presses for urgency, haste, exertion, and diligence. Paul deeply desires Timothy's presence in these horrible circumstances. We might call this a passion for presence. Such is the potential of the disciple investing relationship.

In the area of *pastoral ministry* (teaching/preaching), Paul gives Timothy the following pastoral responsibilities:

1. To prevent the teaching of false doctrine (1.1:3; 1.4:6).
2. To command and teach that people should put their hope in the living God, the Savior of all men, especially those who believe (1.4:11).
3. To provide and insist on the sound instruction of the Lord Jesus Christ, and to provide godly teaching (1.6:2b).
4. To devote himself to the public reading of Scripture, to preaching and to teaching (1.4:13).
5. To guard what has been entrusted to his care and to turn away from godless chatter and the opposing ideas of false knowledge (1.6:20).
6. To keep reminding God's people of these things; to warn them before God against quarreling about words (2.2:14).
7. To do his best to present himself to God as one approved, a worker who does not need to be ashamed and who correctly handles the word of truth; and to avoid godless chatter (2.2:15–16).
8. To preach the word; be prepared in season and out of season; correct, rebuke, and encourage—with great patience and careful instruction (2.4:2).

Observations: Teaching Ministry

True disciple investing is marked by the passing on of sound doctrine, with the effect that the same sound doctrine is passed on by others. The well-discipled individual will avoid anything that smacks of false teaching or doctrine. This avoidance is what Paul, speaking to Timothy the pastor, terms "guarding." As a teaching pastor, Timothy must make every effort to correctly handle Scripture, to publicly read, preach, and teach the Scriptures, to constantly remind people of God's perspective, and to patiently and carefully instruct God's people through correction, rebuke, and encouragement. Surely Timothy watched Paul exhibit these traits in their ministry travels together and understood the poignancy of these instructions:

1. To guide people in how to conduct themselves in the local church thus having nothing to do with godless myths and old wives' tales (1.3:15; 1.4:7).
2. To set an example for the believers in speech, in conduct, in love, in faith, and in purity, despite the fact he is young (1.4:12).
3. To entrust the things Timothy has heard Paul say in the presence of many witnesses to reliable people who will also be qualified to teach others (2.2:2).
4. To not have anything to do with foolish and stupid arguments, because he knows they produce quarrels. And as the Lord's servant, he must not be quarrelsome but must be kind to everyone, able to teach, not resentful. Opponents must be gently instructed (2.2:23–24).
5. To keep his head in all situations, to endure hardship, to do the work of an evangelist, to discharge all the duties of his ministry (2.4:5).

Observations: Pastoral Ministry

Paul wants Timothy to be a guide (or counselor in the classic, biblical sense) to the members of his congregation so that they may conduct themselves properly among the body of Christ, the church. One vital means to providing this guidance is modeling, i.e., demonstrating, how to speak, live, and be an example in personal virtues. Timothy must invest in other disciples, most probably future church leaders who can also invest in others. And in the midst of all of the church tensions which exist between church members, be a wise pastor who should avoid foolish arguments and quarrels. His life and behavior toward others must foster kindness, gentleness toward detractors, peacefulness, and thoughtful resolution through "teachable moments" with his flock. This pastor must be calm and circumspect (sober, "keep his head") in all situations. In a practical sense, he must be level-headed and he must expect and endure hardship. He should never forget the Great Commission of Christ and be an evangelist. He should never lapse in his expected pastoral duties.

In the area of *personal sanctification (spiritual growth)*, Paul exhorts Timothy . . .

1. To fight the battle well, holding on to the faith and a good conscience (1.1:18–19).

2. To train himself to be godly (1.4:7).

3. To flee from all this (false teaching, controversies, and the love of money) and pursue righteousness, godliness, faith, love, endurance, gentleness, and to fight the good fight of the faith (1.6:11–12).

4. To flee the evil desires of youth and pursue righteousness, faith, love and peace, along with those who call on the Lord out of a pure heart (2.2:22).

Observations: Personal Sanctification

Timothy (and all believers) must understand that the Christian life is an active warfare and a good one in which to engage. He must hold on to the faith he has been taught, recognizing that it will be challenged. He must further live in the realm of good and evil, holding on to his sense of good as a guide to his conscience. Being involved in the battle of the faith means that he must discipline himself in order to be godly. Much will come his way to distract him from obedient, holy living.

In the area of *personal discipline and admonition*, Paul tells Timothy . . .

1. To be diligent in matters of public reading of Scripture, preaching, teaching, and the using of his gifts; to give himself wholly to them (1.4:15).

2. To watch his life and doctrine closely and persevere in them (1.4:16).

3. To fight the good fight of faith and take hold of the eternal life to which he was called when he made his good confession in the presence of many witnesses, and to keep this command without spot or blame until the appearing of our Lord Jesus Christ (1.6:12–14).

4. To fan into flame the gift of God, that is in him through the laying on of Paul's hands (2.1:6).

5. To not be ashamed of the testimony about the Lord or of Paul, the Lord's prisoner. Rather, to join with Paul in suffering for the gospel, by the power of God (2.1:8).

6. To be strong in the grace that is from Christ Jesus (2.2:1).

7. To keep what he has heard from Paul as the pattern of sound teaching, with faith and love in Christ Jesus. And to guard the good deposit that was entrusted to him—to guard it with the help of the Holy Spirit who lives in them (2.1:13–14); to join with Paul in suffering, like a good soldier of Christ Jesus (2.2:3).

8. To continue in what he has learned and that of which he has become convinced (2:3:14).

Observations: Personal Discipline and Admonition

Paul cannot accept anything less than all-out effort. If Timothy has gifts, he should take care (literally "take pains") both in using those gifts and in his preaching. He should be "all in" in the matters of ministry! He must maintain (or "hold fast to") the careful balance of living the life and thinking biblical thoughts, and persevere in these endeavors. He must agonize (fight) the good agony of the faith (an allusion to the Greek games, as Paul is in Corinth) and like a true competitor, lay hold onto (grasp the victor's wreath) eternal life. He must keep the command that Paul has laid forth in the letter, fighting the good fight and looking to his life and doctrine. He must not let the gift of ordained ministry (probably referencing the "commendation" of the church/elders in Lystra as recorded in Acts 16:4 and referred to in 1 Timothy 4:14) wane in his life.[7] Like a fire needing kindling, he must keep it burning and not allow his zeal to lag.

He must not be ashamed of Paul's imprisonment, as discouraging and embarrassing as that might be, nor of Jesus, both of whom have suffered. Instead, he must join them in gospel suffering! Timothy must never, ever forget God's grace. He therefore must find his strength for ministry and Christian living in this powerful doctrine of assurance. He must keep the sound doctrine that Paul has passed on to him, while maintaining faith and love in Christ. He must keep the good deposit (the gospel or the sound doctrine taught him) and continue in what he has learned from Paul and has become convinced is true. Effort, vigor, zeal, and focus must emanate

---

7. Bruce, *Acts*, 323.

APPENDIX TWO

from the true disciple of Jesus—it did from Paul; it must also from Timothy . . . and from you and me!

Titus and Pauline Admonitions

Pastoral Epistles

The nature of a brief study such as this one forbids a full commentary on Paul's pastoral epistle written to Titus but, like the treatment of the pastoral letters to Timothy, I would like to take a few moments to survey these writings in order to scan the nature of the Paul/Titus ministerial relationship and how Paul exhorts this younger local church pastor. Since Titus is ministering in the Cretan context, a quote describing the church at Crete might be helpful:

> The situation in Crete was discouraging. The church was disorganized, and its members were quite careless in behavior. If the injunctions in chapter 2 are any indication of what the churches needed, the men were lax and careless, the older women were gossips and winebibbers, and the younger women were idle and flirtatious.[8]

Here is a listing of pastoral admonitions to Titus:

- **Titus 1:5**—"This is why I left you in Crete, so *that you might put what remained into order, and appoint elders in every town* as I directed you."

- **Titus 1:10–16**—"For there are many who are insubordinate, empty talkers and deceivers, especially those of the circumcision party. ¹¹ *They must be silenced, since they are upsetting whole families by teaching for shameful gain what they ought not to teach.* ¹² One of the Cretans, a prophet of their own, said, "Cretans are always liars, evil beasts, lazy gluttons." ¹³ This testimony is true. *Therefore rebuke them sharply, that they may be sound in the faith,* ¹⁴ *not devoting themselves to Jewish myths and the commands of people who turn away from the truth.* ¹⁵ To the pure, all things are pure, but to the defiled and unbelieving, nothing is pure; but both their minds and their consciences are defiled. ¹⁶ They profess to know God, but they deny him by their works. They are detestable, disobedient, unfit for any good work."

---

8. Tenney, *Survey*, 336.

- **Titus 2:1–2**—"*But as for you, teach what accords with sound doctrine. ² Older men are to be sober-minded, dignified, self-controlled, sound in faith, in love, and in steadfastness.*"
- **Titus 2:3–5**—"*Older women likewise are to be reverent in behavior, not slanderers or slaves to much wine. They are to teach what is good, ⁴ and so train the young women to love their husbands and children, ⁵ to be self-controlled, pure, working at home, kind, and submissive to their own husbands, that the word of God may not be reviled.*"
- **Titus 2:6–8**—"*Likewise, urge the younger men to be self-controlled. ⁷ Show yourself in all respects to be a model of good works, and in your teaching show integrity, dignity, ⁸ and sound speech that cannot be condemned, so that an opponent may be put to shame, having nothing evil to say about us.*"
- **Titus 2:15**—"*Declare these things; exhort and rebuke with all authority. Let no one disregard you.*"
- **Titus 3:1–2**—"*Remind them to be submissive to rulers and authorities, to be obedient, to be ready for every good work, ² to speak evil of no one, to avoid quarreling, to be gentle, and to show perfect courtesy toward all people.*"
- **Titus 3:3–8**—"*For we ourselves were once foolish, disobedient, led astray, slaves to various passions and pleasures, passing our days in malice and envy, hated by others and hating one another. 4 But when the goodness and loving kindness of God our Savior appeared, ⁵ he saved us, not because of works done by us in righteousness, but according to his own mercy, by the washing of regeneration and renewal of the Holy Spirit, ⁶ whom he poured out on us richly through Jesus Christ our Savior, ⁷ so that being justified by his grace we might become heirs according to the hope of eternal life. ⁸ The saying is trustworthy, and I want you to insist on these things, so that those who have believed in God may be careful to devote themselves to good works. These things are excellent and profitable for people.*"
- **Titus 3:9–11**—"*But avoid foolish controversies, genealogies, dissensions, and quarrels about the law, for they are unprofitable and worthless. ¹⁰ As for a person who stirs up division, after warning him once and then twice, have nothing more to do with him, ¹¹ knowing that such a person is warped and sinful; he is self-condemned.*"

- **Titus 3:12-15**—"When I send Artemas or Tychicus to you, *do your best to come to me at Nicopolis,* for I have decided to spend the winter there. ¹³ *Do your best to speed Zenas the lawyer and Apollos on their way; see that they lack nothing.* ¹⁴ And let our people learn to devote themselves to good works, so as to help cases of urgent need, and not be unfruitful. ¹⁵ All who are with me send greetings to you. *Greet those who love us in the faith.*"

As we observe Paul's personal letter to his friend and co-worker Titus, we are able to draw some interesting conclusions. I will simply list some of the observations:

In the realm of *personal relationship*, Paul urges Titus . . .

1. To do his best to come to him at Nicopolis (3:12); Paul is probably in Philippi at this writing but wants to meet Titus in a central location. Nicopolis is a Roman colony and a good spot to spend the winter in the non-traveling months of cold and stormy weather. But Titus must not come until Paul's pastoral reinforcements arrive in the person of either Artemas or Tychicus.
2. To assist Zenas the lawyer and Apollos on their way and to be sure they have what they need (apparently in order to travel to some unknown destination (3:13).
3. To greet those believers who love Paul and his companions (3:15).

Observations: Personal Relationship

The epistle to Titus is long on instructions and admonitions and short on relational material. Paul's method of writing in this manner makes sense with Titus since Titus is in a tough spot but is also a strong leader. The letter probably also demonstrates that Paul is not as close to Titus as he is to Timothy. Most likely, Titus also does not need the personal touch in order to motivate or console him in his circumstances. Paul, as with Timothy in his second letter, does want to see Titus personally, so much so that he lobbies for a meeting location that consists of a middle ground for both of them. Their love for each other is seen in Paul's short final words. Possibly Paul knows that Titus's eagerness to see him could be quite compelling, so he encourages him not to come immediately, leaving the Cretan flock behind, but to wait on the reinforcement/substitute pastor that he is going to send. The personal concern Paul has for others and their care is seen in his request to Titus to assist Zenas and Apollos. At the same time, the confidence he has in Titus's conscientiousness is seen in the very fact that he makes such a request.

Finally, Paul's large heart is noticeable as he asks Titus, I believe in a non-perfunctory manner, to greet those who love him and his support team.

In the area of *pastoral ministry,* Paul gives Titus these pastoral responsibilities:

- Teaching and Preaching Ministry: to teach what is appropriate in sound doctrine and to teach the older men to be temperate, worthy of respect, self-controlled, and sound in faith, in love, and in endurance; also, to teach the older women to be reverent in the way they live, not to be slanderers or addicted to much wine, but to teach what is good (2:1–3).

- To demonstrate the following qualities in his teaching: integrity, seriousness, and soundness of speech that cannot be condemned, so that those who oppose him may be ashamed because they have nothing bad to say about him (2:7–8).

- To teach the things he should, i.e., that the grace of God teaches believers to say "No" to ungodliness and worldly passions, and to live self-controlled, upright, and godly lives in this present age, while waiting for the blessed hope—the appearing of the glory of the great God and Savior, Jesus Christ, who gave himself for his people to redeem them from all wickedness and to purify for himself a people that are his very own, eager to do what is good (2:11–14).

Observations: Teaching Ministry

As expected, Paul enjoins Titus to teach sound doctrine and to include integrity and seriousness to his words of instruction. Such instruction will maintain the reputation of the church in view of her opposition. Paul also charges him to teach the older men and women to live in a manner appropriate to their respective gender. And as he closes his letter he reminds Titus to focus on teaching the grace of God because ultimately, understanding grace leads to both purity and goodness.

- Pastoral Ministry: to put in order what was left unfinished and to appoint elders in every town (1:5).
- To silence rebellious people, especially those of the circumcision group, because they are disrupting whole households by teaching things they ought not to teach (1:11).
- To rebuke the Cretan believers sharply, so that they will be sound in the faith and will pay no attention to Jewish myths or to the merely human commands of those who reject the truth (1:13–14).
- To encourage the young men to be self-controlled (2:6).
- To encourage and rebuke with all authority; to not let anyone despise him (2:15).
- To remind the people to be subject to rulers and authorities, to be obedient, to be ready to do whatever is good, to slander no one, to be peaceable and considerate, and to always be gentle toward everyone (3:1–2).
- To stress these things (i.e., that, having been justified by his grace, they might become heirs having the hope of eternal life), so that those who have trusted in God may be careful to devote themselves to doing what is good (3:7–8).
- To avoid foolish controversies, genealogies, arguments, and quarrels about the law, because these are unprofitable and useless (3:9).
- To warn a divisive person once, and then warn them a second time. After that, to have nothing to do with them (3:10).

Observations: Pastoral Ministry

Paul is frank about Titus's job in Crete. It won't be easy; the natives of the island live in a culture that is unconducive to ministry; they are uncooperative and lazy (and evil, although hopefully this is not true of the church members). He must squash the influence of the rebellious Judaizers (who do not fully relish the doctrine of grace). Because of the nature of the citizens of Crete, they must be handled strongly, rebuked sharply, and avoid Jewish myths that would move them away from the faith. They must also avoid foolish and useless controversies, etc., about the law. Apparently, they are easily distracted by matters outside of the periphery of gospel proclamation. Nevertheless (and demonstrating the ministry style of Paul as well) in addition to rebuke, encouragement also is in order, particularly with the young men. This encouragement must be with a proper air of authority, yet must not be with an authority so strong that it would cause others to despise Titus.

Titus's big job encompasses reminding these obstinate believers that they must understand all types of behaviors that impact relationships, from top to bottom in their world. In both categories of teaching and pastoral ministry, Paul places an overemphasis on goodness. This focus would make sense if indeed Cretans are prone to evil (Titus 1:12). Finally, Paul gives some of the best advice any pastor can hear. With the desire for Titus to maintain his pastoral authority (and giving much apparent credibility to it), he tells Titus to warn the divisive person, not just once, but twice and then, in essence, to ignore them. Well said, Paul!

Overall, we note that Paul spends far greater time on the pastoral side of the ministry than the teaching side. Titus has his hands full with the needs of people who have been converted out of a very pagan society. Paul and Titus are both viewed as strong leaders; nevertheless, we can see that Paul is investing in Titus with a lengthy letter of pastoral instruction. Both men have served the gospel with able and capable leadership. However, Paul's letter displays the apostolic authority and respect to which Titus will defer when pastoral problems arise in Crete.

In the area of *personal sanctification*, Paul exhorts Titus . . .

- To set an example to the young men in everything by doing what is good (2:7).

Observations: Personal Sanctification

In some ways, this simple and singular admonition in the area of personal sanctification is comprehensive. Paul mandates the necessity to set an example in everything because the younger men (who may take over the church as they mature and as Titus moves on) are watching and being impacted. Nothing can be compromised. Goodness in "all of life" is the far-reaching admonition from the hand of the beloved friend and gospel comrade and that says it all.

Finally, I close this study of Paul and Titus by once more quoting Dr. William Hendriksen, who helps us wrap up this section with a perceptive description of Titus:

> He loved the Corinthians. He loved his Lord. He loved the work of the Lord, and gave ample evidence of this in the spontaneous manner in which he shouldered his task at Corinth. He breathed the spirit of Paul, and followed closely in his steps (2 Corinthians 12:18). He was original, tactful, courageous, loyal, a close and trusted friend of the great apostle, the latter's true representative in the cause of Christ.[9]

No better summary could capture the mutual passion for Christ and his kingdom that these two disciple investors reflected in their service with and on behalf of one another. Two men, one heart for Jesus!

---

9. Hendriksen, Pastoral, 38–9.

Bibliography

Bruce, F.F. *The Book of Acts*. TNICT. Grand Rapids: Eerdmans, 1954.
Gaebelien, Frank E. *2 Timothy*. The Expositor's Bible Commentary: Vol. 11. Grand Rapids: Zondervan, 1978.
Hendriksen, William. *Exposition of I and II Thessalonians*. NTC. Grand Rapids: Baker, 1955.
———. *Exposition of Philippians*. NTC. Grand Rapids: Baker, 1962.
———. *Exposition of the Pastoral Epistles*. NTC. Grand Rapids: Baker, 1957.
Jamieson, Robert, et al. *A Commentary on the Old and New Testaments*. Vol. III. Peabody: Hendrickson, 1997.
Loesch, Richard. *All the People in the Bible: An A-Z Guide to the Saints, Scoundrels, and Other Characters in Scripture*. Grand Rapids: Eerdmans, 2008.
Ramsay, Sir William. *The Bearing of Recent Discovery on the Trustworthiness of the New Testament*. London: Hodder and Stoughton, 1915.
Spence, H. D. M., and Joseph S. Exell, eds. *Romans*. The Pulpit Commentary: Vol. 18. J Barmby, McLean: MacDonald, 1985.
Spence, H. D. M., and Joseph S. Exell, eds. *II Corinthians*. The Pulpit Commentary: Vol. 19. F. W. Farrar, McLean: MacDonald, 1978.
Tenney, Merrill C. *New Testament Survey*. Grand Rapids: Eerdmans, 1961.

www.ingramcontent.com/pod-product-compliance
Lightning Source LLC
Chambersburg PA
CBHW070932160426
43193CB00011B/1670